BLISTERS
AND
BLISS

A TREKKER'S GUIDE
TO THE
WEST COAST TRAIL

BY
DAVID FOSTER AND WAYNE AITKEN
ILLUSTRATED BY NELSON DEWEY

Published by B & B Publishing, 4081 San Capri Terrace, Victoria, B.C., Canada V8N 2J6
ISBN 0-938567-27-6

First edition: 1989
Second (revised) edition: 1991
Third (revised) edition:1995
Fourth (revised) edition: 1998

Illustration of 'Early Trekker' was printed in the West Coast Trail Information Centre's Report, 1972.

ACKNOWLEDGMENTS

The West Coast Trail is a world-class trekking experience made all the more enjoyable by the contributions of the people who are continuously a part of it. We salute the crew of the M. V. Lady Rose, the lightstation keepers at Pachena and Carmanah Points, the ferry operators at Nitinat Narrows and Port Renfrew. A tip of the old backpack goes to all the folks at Parks Canada who maintain the trail. Particular thanks go to the Quu'as West Coast Trail Group, Reception Centre people and of course the excellent carpenters. In addition we thank the Coast Guard and members of the native bands along the way for helping trekkers in distress and for their patience and caring.

Others who have made Blisters and Bliss possible over the years are Colleen Earl, Carolyn Mellor, Rita Button, Sally Larrington; Norm, Nora and Luke Smith; Carl Edgar Jr. and Matthew; Janet, Jerry, Jake and Justine Etzkorn; Kathy Doyle and Ian, and the incredible number of wonderful characters we have met along the trail.

Hope we are still friends!

This book is dedicated to our wives, Joan and Minna, who for years have tolerated our annual treks, smoky equipment and repetitious telling of our tales. We must be doing something right during the off-season.

-David and Wayne

"I wish I had known about the ladders."

-Wide-eyed Swedish Trekker

"You look down at your boots a lot; write about what you see down there."

-Mary Lea, Massachusetts, USA

"I once saw a man carrying a 70 lb. pack on his back and an 18 month old baby on his chest. His young wife was transporting a large box of Pampers. People who hike the trail should be better prepared than that."

- Norm Smith, Port Renfrew, B.C.

"When the foggy season arrives and the horn kicks in, we can only hold 45 second conversations until the skies clear."

-Janet and Jerry Etzkorn
Carmanah Lightstation Keepers

"Wayne who?"

-Minna Aitken, watching the home fires after
Wayne's fifteenth lucky hike along the Trail.

"It might take 24 hours or a week to hike the West Coast Trail, however, you need to know that after five days, I stop watering the garden at home."

-Joan Foster, watching the home fires after
Dave's fifteenth lucky hike along the Trail.

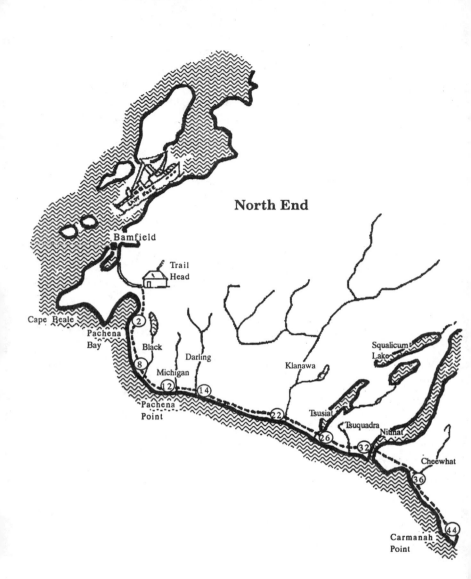

North End

Bamfield

Trail Head

Cape Beale

Pachena Bay

Black

Michigan

Darling

Klanawa

Squalicum Lake

Pachena Point

Tsusiat

Tsuquadra

Nitinat

Cheewhat

Carmanah Point

2

8

12

14

22

26

32

36

44

4

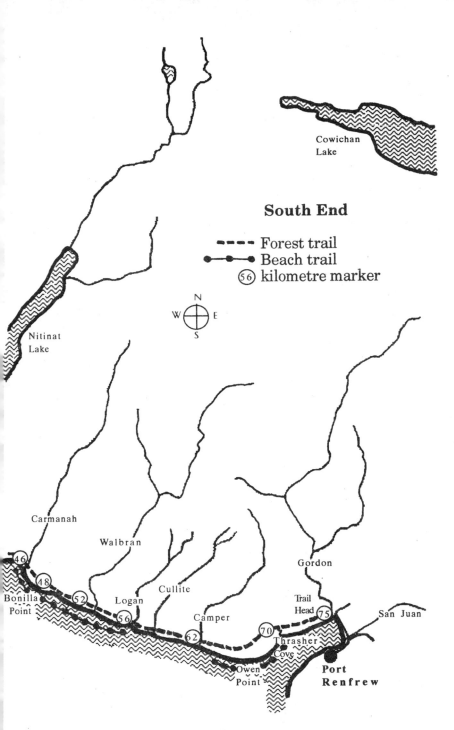

Cowichan Lake

South End

- - - - Forest trail
●━━━●━━━● Beach trail
⑤⑥ kilometre marker

N
W ⊕ E
S

Nitinat Lake

Carmanah

Walbran

Gordon

④⑥
④⑧
Bonilla Point
⑤②
Logan
Cullite
Trail Head
⑤⑥
⑥②
Camper
⑦⑤
San Juan
⑦⓪
Thrasher Cove
Port Renfrew
Owen Point

5

CONTENTS

MAPS:

INTRODUCTION

Each year thousands of trekkers tackle the 75 km West Coast Trail between Bamfield and Port Renfrew on Vancouver Island. Of these, hundreds come from other countries, many are repeat performers and no one forgets the experience.

Hiking the West Coast Trail, as with any world-class trek, can be a time of immense pleasure or exhausting agony. The difference is usually in the amount of care taken in planning and preparing for the trip.

Volumes have been written on backpacking techniques, so we do not intend this to be another "How To" digest. Nor do we want to explain what you will find around every corner, mud hole or ladder. We leave that magic for you to discover. Instead, we have tried to give you a sensible overview of the key areas of interest, trouble spots and distances.

We have written this guide in a manner that describes sections of the trail, so it doesn't matter which direction you are heading. The commentary makes sense both ways (we hope). We have included a number of tips for novices and trail masters alike. They are to support our main goal of providing a safe and practical guide to the West Coast Trail.

We hope Blisters and Bliss will make your adventure safer and more enjoyable. We would love to hear your comments. You can write to us c/o the publishers, or send email to:
Wayne Aitken <wtaitken@home.com>.

If you pack a lot of common sense along with your moleskin and trail mix, you will have a wonderful time. When you see us along the way, stop around for some cowboy coffee, and tell us your story.

- DAVID FOSTER and WAYNE AITKEN

CONDITIONS AFFECTING THE TRAIL ARE CONSTANTLY CHANGING! THE AUTHORS HAVE ATTEMPTED TO VERIFY AND UPDATE THEIR INFORMATION, BUT CANNOT GUARANTEE ITS ACCURACY.

HISTORY OF THE TRAIL

Construction of what is now known as the West Coast Trail began in 1889. It was originally part of an international communication system called the "Red Route." The system connected the British Empire in North America by an undersea cable which ran from Bamfield to India, via Suva in Fiji.

A part of this telegraph network ran down the west coast of Vancouver Island. It connected lightstations at Cape Beale and Carmanah Point with other lightstations and towns toward Victoria. The original trail, therefore, was constructed by telegraph linesmen who strung and maintained lines.

The communcation route ran past the museum in Sooke where you can still see part of the original line.

"..unrecognizable 'things'..."

The region was christened "Graveyard of the Pacific" for good reason. Over fifty ships have gone to rest here during the past one hundred years—nearly one per kilometre. Bits and pieces of many of these ships remain strewn along the coast. The huge boiler of the Michigan, that went down in 1893 at M i c h i g a n Creek, is still visible at low tide. Anchors, capstans, overturned hulls and unrecognizable "things" from other ships are also common.

On January 22, 1906, the passenger ship S.S. Valencia went down on a rocky reef approximately 9 km south of Pachena Point. One hundred and twenty six passengers and crew perished with her. The trail was substantially improved in 1907 to assist survivors of the many shipwrecks which have occurred along this rugged shore. It then became known as the "Life Saving Trail."

From 1907 to 1912 workers cleared the trail and widened it to four metres between Bamfield and Pachena Point. The rugged terrain made the 4 metre width impractical to build between Pachena and

Carmanah Point, so the width was reduced to 1.5 metres over this section. The primitive telegraph trail continued beyond Carmanah to Port Renfrew.

Evidence of some of the equipment that was used to either clear the trail or assist in bygone logging operations still exists. Look for an old "donkey" steam engine and grader between Billygoat and Trestle creeks. A larger engine and several metres of stretched cable are easily noticed on the trail between Thrasher Cove and Gordon River.

Modern technology, such as radio telephones and helicopters made the Life Saving Trail obsolete. Maintenance on the trail stopped in 1954, except between Pachena Point and Bamfield. Salal, salmon berry and branching evergreens soon invaded.

In 1969, with plans to include this region in the third phase of the development of the Pacific Rim National Park, Canadian Parks Service sent in several crews to re-open the trail. There were tense times while park boundaries were being defined.

Conservationists and logging companies went head-to-head in a campaign to have their interests protected. While the two groups continue to have disagreements, each year the trail is maintained and improved. Today we have a world class hiking trail, thanks, in part, to both the Sierra Club and the Canadian Parks Service.

The trail has improved greatly since the early 1970's when ladders were scarce and bridges an endangered species. We are constantly amazed at the high quality of new ladders and landings that have been constructed along the route.

Today, thousands of people use the trail. Registrations peaked in 1990 with over 9,300 trekkers checking in. As a result, visitors began to raise concerns about crowding and undesirable impacts on park resources. Parks Canada introduced a quota and a

reservation system in response to those concerns. The quota limits the overall annual use to about 8,000 hikers from May 1 until September 30. A maximum of 52 may start each day: 26 hikers from the Pachena Bay trailhead and 26 from Gordon River near Port Renfrew.

WHO ARE THE TREKKERS?

For those who get off on statistics here are a few for your files. Parks Canada advises that about 80% of the people they surveyed in 1997 were first-time hikers. Canadians account for 76% of the hikers. German interest is strong at 11%, and US residents make up a further 6%.

The average group size is 3.1 people. (The few .1 people that we have met along the trail have been very pleasant, but a little weary from trying to climb over the mushroom caps.)

Since 1991 the West Coast Trail has been a "dog-free zone." Leave Fido at home to guard your place, while you enjoy a do-do-free trek in one of the best hiking areas in the world.

ABOUT THE RESERVATION SYSTEM

A reservation system was started in 1992 to restrict the number of people who are allowed to hike the trail each day. While it is not essential for you to have a reservation, without one, some people wait for days to get on the trail. The current cost is $25.00 per trekker. Reservations are accepted beginning March 1. Starting in

1998, reservable spaces are only available 3 months in advance. For example, if you want to start hiking August 15, the earliest you can reserve is May 15 (3 months beforehand) We suggest that you make your reservation as close to the available date as you can. They go fast! Currently the number to call is: 1-800-663-6000.

If you live in Vancouver, the number to call is 663-6000.

You will receive a pre-hike information kit from Parks Canada when you phone in your reservation.

TRAIL USE PERMIT FEES

There is a user fee for all hikers. Since the 1998 trekking season, the cost for a permit has been $95.00 per person. This fee includes a $25.00 water taxi fee. Water taxis are needed to cross the Nitinat Narrows and the Gordon River. Fees are collected at the Hiker Reception Centres prior to starting. This will take a significant bite out of everyone's pocket book, but maintenance costs are high. A Parks Canada representative told us, "The intent here is to shift some of the trail cost from the taxpayer to the person who benefits the most - the user". Only hikers displaying a valid Trail Use Permit will be granted passage across the Nitinat Narrows and the Gordon River. Carry your's in a safe place. Further information can be obtained from Parks Canada, (250) 726-7721.

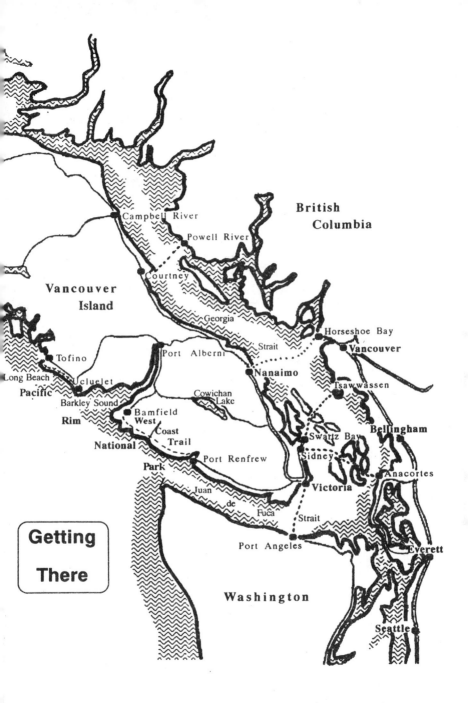

Campbell River

Powell River

British
Columbia

Courtney

Vancouver
Island

Georgia

Horseshoe Bay

Strait

Vancouver

Port Alberni

Tofino

Nanaimo

Tsawwassen

Long Beach

Ucluelet

Pacific

Cowichan
Lake

Barkley Sound

Bamfield
West

Bellingham

Rim

Coast
Trail

Swartz Bay

National

Sidney

Port Renfrew

Anacortes

Park

Victoria

Juan

de

Fuca

Strait

Everett

Port Angeles

Getting

There

Washington

Seattle

A WORD TO THE WISE

The Parks Canada service staff have provided tremendous assistance in completing this book. They offer the following comments:

> *"The West Coast Trail once had the reputation of being one of the most grueling treks in North America and as such it attracted rugged and experienced individuals. In recent years, with its reputation seemingly forgotten, the West Coast Trail has seen a tremendous increase in hiker use. An alarming number of these are first time or novice hikers. Not surprisingly there has been a dramatic increase in the number of injuries occurring on the trail.*
> *Remember that, despite trail improvements, once you step off the boardwalk, the West Coast Trail is the same trek that it used to be. It is an isolated, prolonged and strenuous trek, that is physically challenging and potentially hazardous."*

GETTING THERE

Vancouver Islanders frequently bemoan the hassles they endure in getting to and from the mainland. Visiting trekkers should be prepared for this. Victoria has an international airport for those flying to the Island. The most popular means, however, is to arrive by boat.

"...the most popular means is by boat..."

B.C. Ferries operate year-round passenger services from Tsawwassen, near the south end of Vancouver, to Swartz Bay, near Victoria. Another important route carries passengers from Horseshoe Bay, north of Vancouver, to Nanaimo, near the mid-point of Vancouver Island. Nanaimo is closer to the Bamfield end of the trail. B.C. Ferries leave on the odd hours from 7:00 a.m. to 9:00 p.m. throughout the year. During the busy period, from late June to early September, they run hourly. The trip, which takes approximately one and a half hours, will give you plenty of time to enjoy a bowl of clam

chowder, and marvel over the spectacular scenery. The *Victoria Clipper* sails twice daily between Seattle, Washington and Victoria. The *Coho* ferry brings passengers from Port Angeles, Washington twice daily. *Washington State Ferries* operate between Anacortes and Sidney (near Swartz Bay).

Getting to the trailhead used to present all sorts of challenges. Today, there a dependable shuttle service that will take you there.

The *West Coast Trail Express* links Victoria to Port Renfrew and Bamfield. Both runs leave the front of Island Coach Lines at 7:00 am daily. Return trips leave Port Renfrew at 5:00 pm. and Bamfield at 1:00 pm. The Port Renfrew trip takes about two and a half hours while the trip to Bamfield is at least a four hour adventure, half on dusty, logging roads. Bus service operates between:

  Victoria and Port Renfrew
  Port Renfrew, Nitinat and Bamfield
  Victoria and Bamfield
  Nanaimo and Bamfield
  Port Alberni and Bamfield

Complete information is posted on the West Coast Trail Express website at: *trailbus.com* or at *pacificcoast.net/~wcte*.
Phone numbers are listed on page 93.

THE SOUTH END

Trekkers who do not take the shuttle services must travel to Port Renfrew via Victoria by road, unless they charter a float plane. Since flying is considered to be showing off, we will concentrate only on vehicular means and the "rule of thumb" (i.e. hitch-hiking).

Travel time from Victoria is about 2 to 2 1/2 hours.

There is city bus service from Victoria to Sooke, which is approximately half way to your destination in Port Renfrew. The local bus drivers believe the flat Earth drops off after Sooke, so they turn around and head back for the known world of Victoria. Stranded on the edge of civilization, you have two options: either hitchhike, or catch the West Coast Trail Express.

If you arrive in Sooke in the late afternoon or early evening, and plan to stay for the night, there are campsites at Sunnyshores Marina and the Sooke Flats. Both are located near the Museum and Information Centre. The museum is rich with local history, and the people who work there are always willing to provide information about the area. French Beach Provincial Park, which is about 31 km beyond Sooke on the route to Port Renfrew, also has excellent camping facilities. We have met numerous trekkers who have been trying for hours to hitch a ride, so be prepared for long waits. The best option is to plead with someone you know to drive you to Port Renfrew. You can also do as we have done: drop a car off at Port Renfrew, and bus back to Bamfield for the hike down from the north end. If you want a special adventure, consider taking a boat charter up to Bamfield. More information on these options is available at the Hiker Reception Centre.

THE NORTH END

Hikers starting from the north end may reach Bamfield by vehicle from Port Alberni, or from Victoria via the logging roads that skirt Lake Cowichan, Nitinat and beyond. There are also chartered float planes available at most towns on the island. The road between Port Alberni and Bamfield is very rough and takes a full 2 hours to drive.

One of the most popular means of transportation is by the M.V. Lady Rose. She is a beautiful 1930's vintage cargo and passenger boat that regularly plies the Alberni Inlet, delivering mail and supplies to the inhabitants along the way. At Bamfield, she drops off and picks up her precious load of trekkers.

The Lady Rose has a buddy ship, the Frances Barkley, to share the route between Port Alberni and Bamfield. The Frances Barkley, a 128 ft. vessel, was built in Norway in 1958. In 1990, it sailed from Europe to Port Alberni via the Panama Canal. She now transports anxious trekkers to the trail, or to hot showers, depending on their direction.

The Lady Rose, or the Frances Barkley, cover the distance between Port Alberni and Bamfield on Tuesdays, Thursdays and Saturdays.

Extra sailings are sometimes added on Fridays and Sundays during July and August. Reservations are recommended (see **Travel Connections** at the back of this book).

The trip takes about 4 1/2 hours. It's a wonderful orientation to the west coast. If you can find a better cheeseburger than the ones cooked on the Lady Rose, we want to hear about it. Sailing time is 8:00 a.m. from the Port Alberni Quay.

If you need to spend the night in Port Alberni, try the Dry Creek Campground. It is about a half hour walk from the bus depot and fifteen minutes from the Quay. Get to the dock early to watch the loading. Sample the freshly made donuts and coffee in the little restaurant nearby.

For those with a heartier appetite we recommend the Blue Door Cafe, which is located at the entrance to the Quay. The food is great, the portions substantial, and the ambiance... Service is also prompt and friendly.

18

The Lady Rose leaves Bamfield at approximately 1:30 p.m. and arrives in Port Alberni around 5:30 p.m.

The Lady Rose and Frances Barkley dock at Bamfield East, and then cross the channel to Bamfield West where the journey finally ends for all hikers.

The trailhead is about 5 km over a gravel road from the Bamfield dock. If a van is not at the dock to transport you, stop by the general store, or try Hawkeye's at the end of the dock to inquire about transportation. The stretch of road can be hiked by 'purists' in about an hour, but it is very dusty and unexciting. There is a fabulous campsite on Pachena Beach, which is located at the trailhead.

NITINAT LAKE

There is no longer access to the trail from Nitinat Village, however, you may leave the trail here. A water taxi will take you from the trail at Nitinat Narrows to the town's small dock -- a trip that lasts about 1/2 hour. The current fare is $25.00 per person.

Now that you are at the trailhead, there is only one means of transportation left. You guessed right...

...IT'S TREKKING TIME!!!

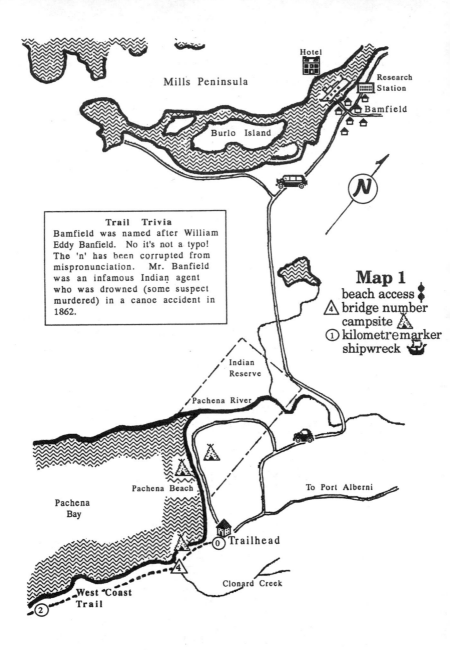

Mills Peninsula

Hotel

Research Station

Bamfield

Burlo Island

Trail Trivia
Bamfield was named after William Eddy Banfield. No it's not a typo! The 'n' has been corrupted from mispronunciation. Mr. Banfield was an infamous Indian agent who was drowned (some suspect murdered) in a canoe accident in 1862.

Map 1
beach access
△₄ bridge number
campsite △
① kilometre marker
shipwreck 🚢

Indian Reserve

Pachena River

Pachena Beach

Pachena Bay

To Port Alberni

△

⓪ Trailhead

△

△₄

Clonard Creek

West Coast Trail

②

20

MAP 1: PACHENA BAY - THE BEGINNING AND END

There are freshwater tanks for those wishing to top up for the push to Pachena Lightstation. This part of your journey takes about three hours of leisurely trekking—two and a half if you are pushing it. Add another hour for the section between Michigan Creek and the Lightstation.

Hikers ending their journey are encouraged to sign out and advise the park attendant of any unusual details that could affect those who are just starting.

Those who are starting must register at the information centre. Its operating hours are 9.00 a.m. to 5 p.m. from May 1 to September 30. A short video about the trail is shown; litter bags, maps and tide tables are distributed. Current warnings are communicated (bear seen at Orange Juice Creek, cable car out at Walbran, bridge knocked out of commission at Sandstone, etc.), so it is important that you check in before you begin.

Indulge in the toilets. Even with the new c o n v e n i e n c e s installed at every major campsite, these luxuries will still seem few and far between. Please use the toilets only for the purpose they were intended.

If there are no toilets nearby when nature calls, try to do your business below the tide line. We call it "surfing." Find a private place, dig a hole, away you go, cover it up and let the Pacific Ocean do the rest. Stay away from freshwater sources!

We highly recommend Kathleen Meyer's book "How to Shit in the Woods," published by 10 Speed Press. It is a frank and humourous book about a serious topic, and mandatory reading for any trekker.

If you have a quarter handy, you can also use the pay phone, your last means of high-tech communications for awhile. If you are starting here ... happy trails! If you are finishing ... well done! We hope you find a hot shower soon.

Tip:

It's a long 5 km on a dusty road from the trailhead to Bamfield. Ask the Park Attendant, or check the bulletin board near the parking lot for the latest transportation information. For a few dollars, it's worthwhile not to add this stretch to your trek.

"...the road can be hiked..."

INTRODUCING THE NEWEST IDEA IN "MINI-MOTORHOMES"
WALKABAGO

YOU'VE NOTICED THEY'RE MAKING CAMPERS AND MOTORHOMES IN EVERY PRICE-RANGE...AND FOR EVERY TASTE...RIGHT? WELL, THE INDUSTRY HASN'T BEEN CONTENT WITH JUST HIGHWAY HAULERS. IN A BOLD MOVE, THEY'VE COME OUT WITH A CAMPER FOR *HIKERS!*
YOU BACKPACKERS NEEDN'T BE ENVIOUS NOW, WHEN THOSE SELF-CONTAINED RIGS PULL INTO THE NEXT CAMPSITE AND HAS A SIX-COURSE MEAL WHILE *YOU'RE* STILL STRUGGLING WITH YOUR PUP TENT AND TRYING TO HEAT A CAN OF SPAM OVER A *BIC* LIGHTER. THROW ONE OF THESE RIGS ON YOUR BACK AND YOU'LL FACE OL' MOMMA NATURE IN COMFORT THIS SUMMER!

©NELSON DEWEY 88,94

SOME OF WALKABAGO'S FEATURES....

This rig has all the goodies the big ones do! Power Take Off Winch (on the boot)... "Bumper-Mount" trail-skateboard (instead of a heavy-weight trail-*bike*)... Side mirrors for keepin' an eye out for bears (both the legal types *and* the 4-legged types)... A 120-band CB rig (for tellin' everybody else about the bears)... Fully-equipped kitchen and bathroom – and overhead bed (you'll need 'em all! It'll take *days* to get anywhere with this heavy rig!)... But you won't be bored -- just watch the TV (powered by the Onan generator)! *HAPPY HIKING !!!*

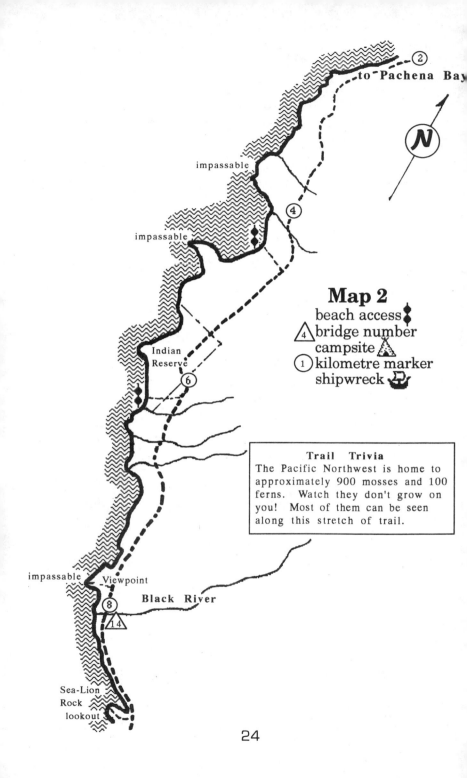

to Pachena Bay

N

impassable

impassable

Map 2
beach access
bridge number
campsite
kilometre marker
shipwreck

Indian
Reserve

Trail Trivia
The Pacific Northwest is home to
approximately 900 mosses and 100
ferns. Watch they don't grow on
you! Most of them can be seen
along this stretch of trail.

impassable   Viewpoint

Black River

Sea-Lion
Rock
lookout

MAP 2: PACHENA BAY TRAILHEAD—BLACK RIVER

APPROXIMATE TREKKING TIME: 2 1/2 - 3 HOURS
DISTANCE: 8 KM

The trail is very well groomed along most of this section. It is removed from ocean views, for the most part, but the woods are wonderful. This is one of the easiest sections of the entire hike. It provides welcome relief for tired southern starters and a nice warm-up for the heavy packers from the north.

Do not be lulled into thinking this is an easy stroll. It is 12 km from Pachena Bay to Michigan Creek, the first campsite for south bounders.

High cliffs and impassable headlands make beach hiking impractical if not impossible in most places. There are *no fires permitted* on the trail between Pachena trailhead and Michigan Creek.

KM 4

Just past KM 4, there is a view point a few meters from the trail. We do not recommend that you go down to the beach at this point. It is too steep for safe climbing. Instead, enjoy the great views here, as well as near KM 6 and KM 8 just north of Black River.

BLACK RIVER

Black River is crossed by bridge. The water has a high mineral content, so do not drink it. There is tap water at both Pachena Point Lightstation and the trailhead.

Tip:

Whenever possible, lean your pack on a log before putting it on or taking it off. The added height from ground level will save wear and tear on your back.

25

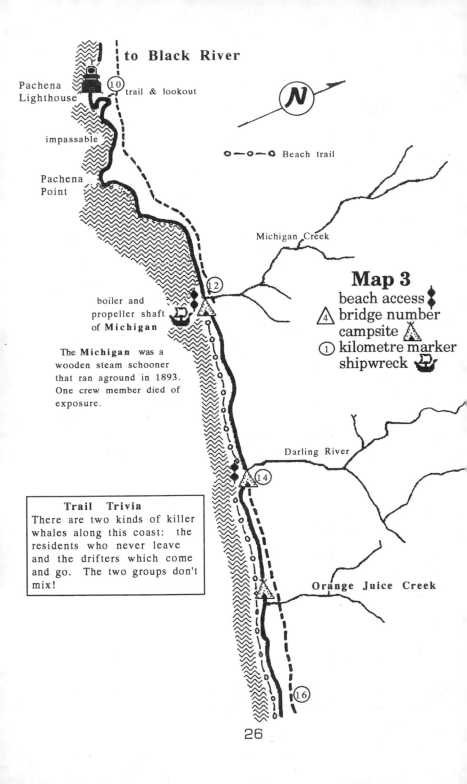

to Black River

Pachena
Lighthouse

trail & lookout

impassable

Pachena
Point

Michigan Creek

boiler and
propeller shaft
of **Michigan**

The **Michigan** was a
wooden steam schooner
that ran aground in 1893.
One crew member died of
exposure.

O—O—O Beach trail

Map 3
beach access ⚲
△4 bridge number
campsite △
①1 kilometre marker
shipwreck ⛵

Darling River

Trail   Trivia
There are two kinds of killer
whales along this coast: the
residents who never leave
and the drifters which come
and go. The two groups don't
mix!

Orange Juice Creek

26

MAP 3: BLACK RIVER - ORANGE JUICE CREEK

APPROXIMATE TREKKING TIME: 2-3 HOURS
DISTANCE: 7.5 KM

PACHENA POINT LIGHTSTATION

Pachena Point Lightstation is about 2 km from Black River and 2 km

from Michigan Creek. Check before entering the grounds. If the grounds are open there are excellent views to enjoy.

If you are lucky, you will see gray whales "doing their thing" off the rocks at the lightstation. We have seen them so close to shore that the noise from their blow holes was clearly audible and their spray nearly watered the lawn!

MICHIGAN CREEK

Michigan Creek is about a half hour beach stroll from Darling River and about one hour via trail from the lightstation.

Michigan has plenty of water, but firewood can be a problem late in the season. This is one of the most heavily used campsites, due to its easy access from the north, and pleasant location. There are plenty of campsites on both sides of the creek. The boiler of the Michigan which ran aground on the shelf in 1893, is clearly visible at low tide. This is an excellent place to admire sunsets and check out tidal pools on hot, clear days. Whales are frequently seen feeding on the shelf.

DARLING RIVER

Darling is easily reached by beach from both Michigan and Orange Juice Creeks. There is a cable car here, but the creek can be waded if you do not mind getting your toes wet. Remember to take your pack off when you use the cable cars. The beach trail is passable at tides below 3.7 M.

Note: At the time of writing, the inside trail between Michigan and Darling is not passable.

Darling has excellent campsites and plenty of water.

ORANGE JUICE CREEK

Orange Juice is about 1.5 km from Darling and is reached either by beach or by trail. We recommend the beach route.

If you are heading south, welcome to beach walking! People coming from Port Renfrew already know this to be a mixed blessing.

Walking close to the water's edge is often easier than near the tide line. It can also be damaging to some marine organisms, especially the small snails in sandstone areas. Please watch your step!

Orange Juice is a wonderful campsite but not as convenient as more popular campsites, so it is often much more private.

Tips:

Look for hanging clusters of old marker buoys. They signify beach access points along the trail.

Wear gaiters, or fold the outside pair of your socks over the top of your boots to help keep sand and blisters out.

Cut the feet off an old pair of long wool socks. Put them over the top of your boots for instant, recycled gaiters. Looks dumb, but it really works.

Walking close to the water's edge is often easier than above the high tide line (the point closest to the trees where you last see seaweed).

Let a strong hiker set the beach trail first, then walk in her foot prints.

If you are a beachcomber, the best place to find flotsam and jetsam is around the high tide logs.

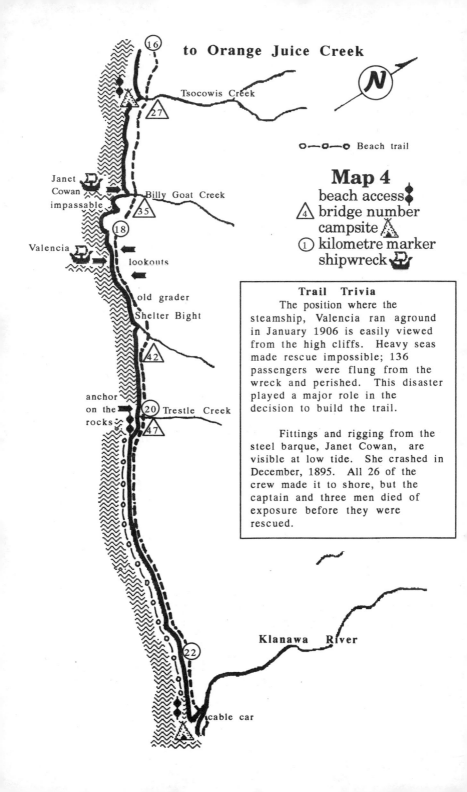

to Orange Juice Creek

Tsocowis Creek

N

○—□—○ Beach trail

Map 4
beach access
△ bridge number
campsite
① kilometre marker
shipwreck

Janet Cowan
impassable

Billy Goat Creek

Valencia

lookouts

old grader

Shelter Bight

anchor on the rocks

Trestle Creek

Klanawa River

cable car

Trail Trivia

The position where the steamship, Valencia ran aground in January 1906 is easily viewed from the high cliffs. Heavy seas made rescue impossible; 136 passengers were flung from the wreck and perished. This disaster played a major role in the decision to build the trail.

Fittings and rigging from the steel barque, Janet Cowan, are visible at low tide. She crashed in December, 1895. All 26 of the crew made it to shore, but the captain and three men died of exposure before they were rescued.

MAP 4: ORANGE JUICE CREEK — KLANAWA RIVER

APPROXIMATE TREKKING TIME: 2 1/2 HOURS
DISTANCE: 8 KM

The terrain along this stretch varies from easy beach trekking at either end, to rugged cliffs with lookouts between Billy Goat and Trestle Creeks. Even on the higher stretches, the trail is well maintained and easily hiked. Most of the terrain is flat along this section, albeit high above the water.   In many places, the inland route is like a stroll to grandma's house.

TSOCOWIS CREEK

There is an excellent campsite next to a waterfall on the north side of Tsocowis. You will find plenty of firewood and water here. A short climb from the beach to the trail takes you to a swinging bridge high above the creek. The view is wonderful. The lookouts between Billygoat and Trestle Creek provide other opportunities to shoot some frames.

An impassable headland near the south side of Billygoat, combined with the steep cliffs of the Valencia Bluffs are fair warning to keep to the inland trail between Tsocowis and the beach access at KM 21.

VALENCIA LOOKOUT

The views from here are unique and overlook the site where the iron steamship "Valencia" went down in heavy seas in 1906. You do not want to be on the beach here under any circumstances.

Tip:

This is a popular place to drop packs and dig into your power bars and trail mix. Be careful where you sit and set your packs. The tree roots at the side of the trail are covered with pitch.

31

Look for the old grader on the trail near the Valencia Lookout. There is also a rusted-out donkey engine close to Shelter Bight. Early trekkers used to run up and down the trail with these strapped on their backs just to keep in shape, or so the story goes.

KM 21

There is a trail access point near KM 21, which is about 1 km south of Trestle Creek. If you are coming from Klanawa, you must go inland here. For those heading south, you have the option of staying on the trail, or hiking the beach route. We recommend the beach, but check that tides are below 3.7 metres before you leave the safety of the trail.

KLANAWA RIVER

The section between Klanawa and KM 21 provides good beach walking, mostly via stone shelf, but with boulders thrown in for good measure. The trail

route is through an extensive spruce grove which is also a fine walk. The trees are magnificent, but the trail may be sloppy.

You should take the cable car at Klanawa, as the water is often high, fast and too dangerous to cross otherwise.

32

If you must wade, keep your hip belts undone on your packs to allow for escape in the event you get dunked. There are campsites by the north side of Klanawa for those who find too much traffic at Tsusiat, approximately 3 km to the south. Access to the cable car at Klanawa is best gained by the beach access which is about 50 M from the river on the north end. The river-edge route is a little more rugged. Branches often extend onto this path and test your good humour.

Stay on the trail between Klanawa and Tsusiat Falls. There are impassable headlands between the beach access at the falls and KM 24.

Tips:

When beach walking, beware of any slimy green stuff that grows on the rocks and hard packed sand—it is very slippery when wet.

Undo hip belts on your pack when crossing surge channels or fast flowing streams. People have drowned trying to get out of their packs.

When climbing ladders, wait until the person ahead of you reaches a landing. The domino effect of falling trekkers is not a pretty sight.

Do not open the fuel cap while your stove is hot. The contents are under pressure and may ignite when you remove the cap.

Treat your drinking water at all times.

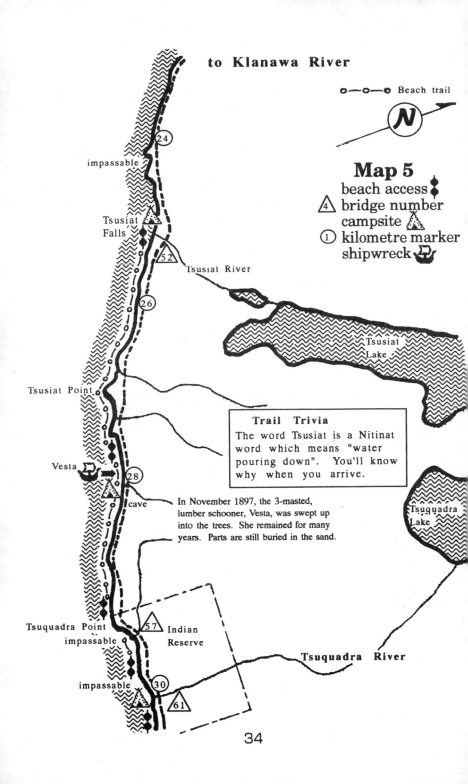

to Klanawa River

o—o—o Beach trail

Map 5
beach access
△4 bridge number
campsite △
① kilometre marker
shipwreck

24

impassable

Tsusiat
Falls

52

Tsusiat River

26

Tsusiat
Lake

Tsusiat Point

Trail Trivia
The word Tsusiat is a Nitinat
word which means "water
pouring down". You'll know
why when you arrive.

Vesta

28

cave

In November 1897, the 3-masted,
lumber schooner, Vesta, was swept up
into the trees. She remained for many
years. Parts are still buried in the sand.

Tsuquadra
Lake

Tsuquadra Point
impassable

57 Indian
Reserve

Tsuquadra River

impassable

30

61

34

MAP 5: KLANAWA RIVER—TSUQUADRA POINT

APPROXIMATE TREKKING TIME: 2 1/2 TO 3 HOURS
DISTANCE: 7KM

The trail from Klanawa River to Tsusiat Falls is all inland. There are a lot of steady and not so steady climbs. For south bound trekkers, this is the start of some impressive ladders.

The north bound route between KM 29 and Tsusiat Falls, can be covered either on the beach or via the inland trail. The trail offers periodic views of the ocean. The beach is spectacular, but the sand is loose and can be hard slogging at the end of a long day in the boots. Near KM 30 there are some remarkable trees.

TSUSIAT FALLS

Tsusiat Falls campsite can be reached by beach from the south and by trail from either the north or south. It is one of the most popular campsites along the entire route.

If you are approaching from the north, do not take the small, unmarked trail that leads to the right immediately after crossing the bridge that spans the river. This path leads to the top of the falls and there is no access to the beach. It is dangerous here, and a drop of about 20 M to the bottom if you slip. Instead, carry on for a few more minutes until you come to the ladders leading to the beach. They are steep and high and will give you enough thrills without jumping off the waterfall.

Tsusiat Falls is a spectacular natural feature that draws thousands of visitors each year. It provides a refreshing opportunity for sunbathers and dusty travelers to clean up and forget about the rigors of the walk for awhile. There are rock shelves to sit on behind the falls, but be careful, they are slippery and can be dangerous.

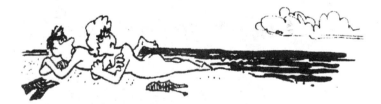

The outstanding beauty of this campground is constantly threatened by its heavy use. Parks Canada has solved part of the problem by providing a luxurious composting toilet. Our role as users is to help keep the sand clean by containing fires and picking up after ourselves. It is no fun having to clean up someone else's mess after sweating it out in the harness all day. We really hope everyone realizes this.

Travel between Tsusiat Falls and Tsusiat Point is an easy beach boogie. Beach access trails are identified near the point by the usual array of coloured floats. Tsusiat Point is passable through the hole in the wall at tides below 2.7 M.

TSUQUADRA POINT

Beach access is located near KM 28. North bound folks can stay on the trail, or hit the sand if the tides are right.

South bounders need to get onto the trail here. The trail passes through an Indian Reservation near KM 30 and Tsuquadra Point is located in this area. Signs are posted to restrict beach access while in this special area. Please respect their message.

There is a campsite in a cave along the trail, midway between Tsusiat and Tsuquadra Points. The cave, which can serve as a foul weather shelter, is approximately 100 square metres with a stand up ceiling. It is noticeable from either direction.

"...a campsite in a cave..."

Much of the trail is flat here and the trees are magnificent. It is well worth staying in the woods.

The trail is much higher between KM 31 and Nitinat Narrows. The views are spectacular - even on dreary days. As you near Nitinat Narrows, the trail dips and heads inland over many boardwalks bridges, ladders and intertwined roots.

Tips:

Load up on water at Tsusiat Falls if heading south or at one of the other sources between the Cribs and Carmanah if heading north. This is a long, "dry" stretch.

Carry tide tables and a watch. Leave yourself plenty of time to trek beach areas where tide levels make a difference.

Use biodegradable soap products to give nature -- and other trekkers, a break.

"...use biodegradable soap.."

If you get caught on the beach or shelf with an incoming tide on one side and steep cliffs an the other, head for the points. The points may slope more gently and there may be old access trails or ropes to get you safely back on the trail.

A log crossing may appear to be safe, but be cautious. They can get very slippery when wet and they may be tilted at slight angles. Injury could literally be as easy as falling off a log.

Conceived over a period of several days, the **F-K A/T HIKING BOOT** is the result of numerous long (and to nearby hikers and campers, quite boring) discussions between two outdoors enthusiasts who should have been watching where they were walking (two words: deer doo-doo). Designed specifically with the West Coast Trail Trekker in mind, this boot has many unique features, including the convertible toe cover (to allow all-over tanning), the toe-grip suction-cup insole, the built-in Global Position Satellite receiver, the "No-Blistr"™ cutaways at sensitive locations, and the "Beach Boogie"™ traction devices on either side of the heel. It's expected these two creative minds will be getting together on the trail again next year and designing yet another piece of footwear, which - in combination with this - will constitute a complete **pair** of hiking boots.

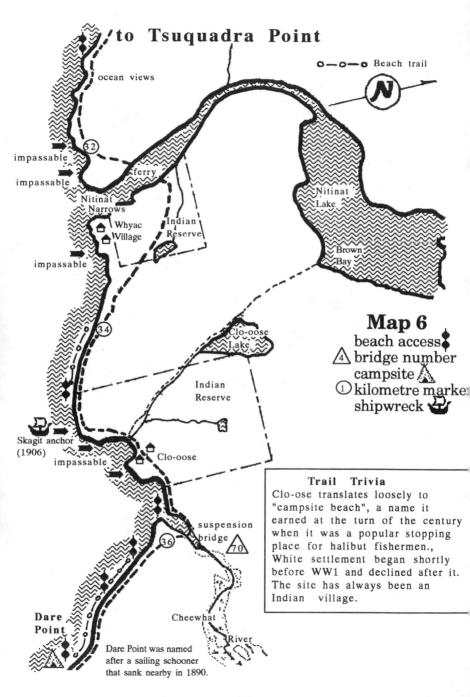

to Tsuquadra Point

o—o—o Beach trail

N

ocean views

impassable

impassable

(32)

ferry

Nitinat
Narrows

Whyac
Village

Indian
Reserve

Nitinat
Lake

impassable

Brown
Bay

(34)

Clo-oose
Lake

Indian
Reserve

Map 6
beach access
△4 bridge number
campsite △
①kilometre marker
shipwreck

Skagit anchor
(1906)

impassable

Clo-oose

suspension
bridge

(36)

△70

Trail Trivia

Clo-ose translates loosely to "campsite beach", a name it earned at the turn of the century when it was a popular stopping place for halibut fishermen., White settlement began shortly before WW1 and declined after it. The site has always been an Indian village.

**Dare
Point**

Cheewhat

River

Dare Point was named
after a sailing schooner
that sank nearby in 1890.

MAP 6: TSUQUADRA POINT—DARE POINT

APPROXIMATE TREKKING TIME: 3.5 HOURS
(Time will vary with availability of ferry service at Nitinat Narrows)
DISTANCE: 8 KM

NITINAT NARROWS

Nitinat Narrows must be crossed by boat. The current runs up to eight knots and the water is cold and deep. The water looks inviting, but it is not drinkable because of the high salt content.

There are magnificent trees growing on the north side of the Narrows and high bluffs offer spectacular views. Be careful on the boardwalk leading to the crossing point.

The ferry operator makes periodic checks for trekkers to take them the short distance across the river. If he is not visible, drop your packs, put your feet up and enjoy the scenery. There is no other option.

Carl Edgar Jr., his family, friends and a wonderful assortment of dogs and kids take trekkers across the narrows in their open fishing boat. There may be fresh seafood available here for reasonable prices. Many a year we've cooked fresh ling cod that was so good it brought tears to our eyes! Dungeness crab is another delight to look for. Liquid treats can also be purchased. Please deposit all empty cans in the bins provided near the dock.

Timing is critical at this point since the ferry service operates between 9:00 a.m. and 5:00 p.m., May 1 to September 30. There are several crossings each day and this is also the departure point for hikers leaving the trail to go to Nitinat Village. Once again, the Nitinat Narrows are always salty. Take care to carry lots of water when you trek this section. In an emergency, there is a small spring 200 M from the south dock. Look for a side trail, it can be easy to miss. Do not rely on getting water here.

CHEEWHAT RIVER

The trail between Nitinat and Cheewhat River is mainly inland along extensive boardwalks that cut across Indian Reservations. Excellent time can be made hiking this stretch, but please be careful if the boards are wet. We both have cedar slat imprints on our butts from slips in bygone years.

Beach access is located near the north end of Clo-oose Reserve, not far from where the Skagit ran aground in 1906. You might not be able to enter this area if the restricted access signs are up. If it is open, look for the anchor on the beach.

A suspension bridge spans the Cheewhat River. It is "user friendly" and sometimes provides shade for raccoons and river creatures.

The Cheewhat is aptly named. We have heard that one translation of "Cheewhat" is ... "River of Urine" - enough said. Hope you brought a good supply of water!

DARE POINT

The section between Cheewhat and Dare Point is one of our favorites. The woods are peaceful, the trail is very wide and level in most places, and the beach — ahhh the beach!

The good news is Dare Beach is about 1 1/2 km of lovely white sand. Bathe your blisters and enjoy!

The bad news is that there is almost no water alonq the entire stretch. There is a small "stream" (read dribble of water) that is right at Dare Point near the most southerly point of the beach. A pool may have to be dug to get enough water for cooking. Take special care to boil or treat this water before drinking.

Note: In 1999 there was a water pump located at KM 37 on the east side of the trail. It may still be operating.

Occasionally, vast flocks of seagulls take over this area. They can do some interesting things to the quality of drinking water in a small stream, so be prepared to move on if they have moved in before you. The Dare Point mouse brigade has claimed squatter's rights on any food that is left open. Hang your pantry high if you are staying near this gang.

Tip:
If you are staying at Dare Point and want to get water from the small stream and have trouble getting enough into your bottle, scoop a hole in the stream bed and line it with a few stones. After the silt settles it should make a fine watering hole.

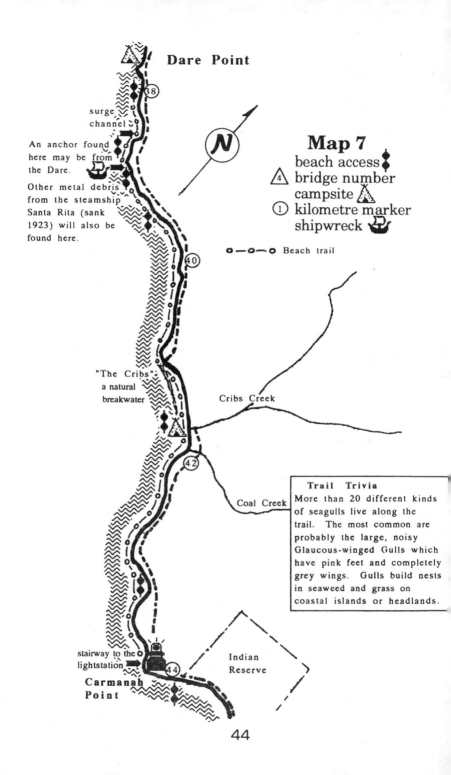

Dare Point

surge
channel

An anchor found
here may be from
the Dare.

Other metal debris
from the steamship
Santa Rita (sank
1923) will also be
found here.

Map 7

beach access
△4 bridge number
campsite △
① kilometre marker
shipwreck

o—o—o Beach trail

38

40

"The Cribs":
a natural
breakwater

Cribs Creek

42

Coal Creek

Trail Trivia
More than 20 different kinds
of seagulls live along the
trail. The most common are
probably the large, noisy
Glaucous-winged Gulls which
have pink feet and completely
grey wings. Gulls build nests
in seaweed and grass on
coastal islands or headlands.

stairway to the
lightstation

Carmanah
Point

44

Indian
Reserve

44

MAP 7: DARE POINT—CARMANAH POINT

APPROXIMATE TREKKING TIME: 21/2 TO 3 HOURS
DISTANCE: 6 KM

This section can be hiked by trail, or, if tides are below 2.7 M., by beach.   The trail route has interesting views - some from high vantage points.   The beach is much more interesting.   If you have trouble deciding, there are several access points along the way.

KM 38 SURGE CHANNEL

There is a difficult surge channel just south of KM 38.   For this reason, we recommend that south bound trekkers take the trail from Dare Beach until at least KM 39.   Then, if the tides are right, you can scoot along to the Cribs, Coal Creek and eventually Carmanah Point.   Those who are heading north along the beach, should look for a steep, short trail that leads up from the shelf at KM 39.   This is the preferred route, rather than risk going down from the shelf and eventually facing the surge channel. The rocks in this area are very slippery.   Tides must be below 2.7 M before you tackle this section. The Santa Rita, which went down in 1923 left its debris along this stretch.   It can do the same to you.   Your safest alternative is to stay on the inland trail.

Tip:

If you insist on going on the beach between KM 39 and Dare Point, look for a grapefruit-sized rock protruding from the north face of the shelf at KM 39. This rock provides the only foothold for getting up or down from the high shelf to the beach.

CRIBS CREEK

Water is seasonally dependent along this route until you get to Cribs or Coal Creeks. There is one other campsite, at KM 40, that may have water. This is a lovely spot and seldom used.

North bound trekkers should top up with water from this area because there is none to rely on between here and Tsusiat Falls.

The Cribs Creek water is better than at Dare but the best is at Carmanah. Increased traffic in the upper Carmanah Valley is

rapidly changing the quality of the river water. It may look great but it must be treated.

The "Cribs," a natural, rocky breakwater, is a unique coastal feature along this stretch. It is easy to hike and the scenery is spectacular. Thousands of sea birds may be resting on these rocks and along the beach. If you walk through the flock, be prepared for a loud and spectacular show of motion. Wear a hat!

Steep cliffs between Dare Point and Cribs Creek block trail access in several places. Be sure of the tide levels and give yourself plenty of time to get through this area. Do not get caught hiking here with water lapping at your feet.

CARMANAH POINT

Most of the time throughout the year there are sea lions off Carmanah Point. You can frequently hear and smell them before you actually see them. Ahhhhh, the west coast!

The stretch between Carmanah Point and the Cribs can be trekked inland, or by beach. Either way is well traveled. We prefer the beach. Carmanah Point is crossed either by trekking the regular trail and bypassing the lightstation or by climbing a long flight of stairs from the beach at the north end. The stairs emerge on the station grounds.

Many trekkers claim that these stairs are twice as high going up as they are going down. Let your body make the call!

Water is available here, but you can also fill up at Carmanah Creek just 2 km to the south. Another flight of stairs lead down to the fabulous beach on the south side. It is located at the north end of the beach about 2 km from Carmanah River campsite.

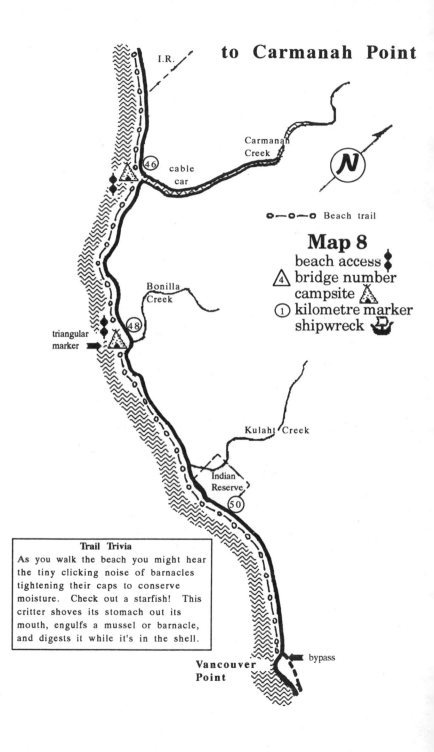

to Carmanah Point

I.R.

Carmanah
Creek

N

46 cable
car

o—o—o Beach trail

Map 8
beach access
bridge number
campsite
kilometre marker
shipwreck

4

1

Bonilla
Creek

triangular
marker

48

Kulaht Creek

Indian
Reserve

50

Trail Trivia
As you walk the beach you might hear
the tiny clicking noise of barnacles
tightening their caps to conserve
moisture. Check out a starfish! This
critter shoves its stomach out its
mouth, engulfs a mussel or barnacle,
and digests it while it's in the shell.

Vancouver
Point

bypass

MAP 8: CARMANAH POINT—VANCOUVER POINT

APPROXIMATE TREKKING TIME: 21/2 TO 3 HOURS
DISTANCE: 7KM

Travel between Carmanah Point and Vancouver Point is all on the beach. There are excellent views along this sandy stretch.

The beach between Carmanah Point and the campsite at Carmanah Creek is a classic. It is about 2 km in length, a beautiful reward for south bounders and an easy walk.

Be sure to stop by Chez Monique's near the north end of the beach. Monique (if her settlement is still occupied) will tell you her story about ancient Native claims to the area. You can buy a soft drink or even a hot dog. She has built a shelter for trekkers who have run into trouble with the weather.

We know of one soggy person who has benefited from Monique's good will. On two occasions, he soaked his borrowed sleeping bag and then burned it trying to dry it. The second year, he burned his own tent! We can only hope for this unfortunate gentleman that it will be "third time lucky."

49

CARMANAH CREEK

Carmanah Creek offers an excellent campsite with plenty of wood, fresh water and postcard-calibre views. The single drawback to this site becomes evident when the fog rolls in. The Carmanah Point Light Station fog horn has the longest series of warning blasts along the coast—three honks every ninety seconds! It can bring tears to the eyes of weary trekkers who have just tucked in at the end of a long day.

Carmanah Creek can be waded near its mouth during July, August and September. Be careful of the strong current. If you are determined to keep dry, use the cable car. Do not go searching up and down the creek (it is more like a river than a creek) looking for a dry crossing, for they are rare. Park your pack, doff your boots and stroll across near the mouth. Your tootsies will thank you.

CARMANAH VALLEY TREES

Carmanah Valley is the home of many of the world's tallest Sitka Spruce. Some of these giants are over 3 M in diameter and are estimated to be more than 700 years old. The tallest tree is nearly thirty-two stories high. We tip our packs to the Heritage Forest Society, Sierra Club and Western Canada Wilderness Committee for their unfaltering effort to save these treasures from chainsaws.

50

BONILLA POINT

Bonilla is easily identified because of a large, red navigation triangle located above the beach. It has a good campsite with plenty of wood and a small waterfall. The trail section is poorly maintained and you are encouraged to trek on the beach. The sand is fine and can make for tough slogging.

"...fine sand makes for tough trekking..."

This is one stretch where gaiters, or spats are handy to keep the pebbles on the beach and out of your boots. Wayne likes to use the "sand-in-the-boots" trick as an excuse to stop. He takes off his boots, shakes out his socks and enjoys the scenery. It drives Dave crazy!

Passage from Bonilla to Vancouver Point is possible when tides are below 3.7 M. There is an overturned logging tug on the shelf near Bonilla. It will reveal its humble interior if you look in the hole on the port side. There are other pieces of long lost ships stuck here and there in the sand. We have seen several river otters around here. One year we watched a dozen seals herd a school of small fish into the shallows at Kulaht as a prelude to a seafood buffet. Deer occasionally wander by. One actually allowed itself to be scratched behind its ears, just like some trekkers!

VANCOUVER POINT

If you are a south-bounder, look for beach access on the north side of Vancouver Point. This trail section will end at the cable car on Walbran Creek about 2 km away.

You may beach boogie between Vancouver Point and Walbran Creek if tides are below 3.7 M and Walbran is not in flood. We recommend this route.

"...the beach boogie..."

DAVE'S ADVICE ON MICE
No other creature will have such a profound affect on your hike as the innocent field mouse.

On a rare, still and sultry night on a west coast beach, we left the tent flap open just a smidgon to make the thick, body-odoured air more tolerable. Late in the night, gentle scratchings and crunchings awakened us. A tiny moving thing scampered across my sleeping bag. Wayne yelled, "The little s.o.b. ran across my face!"

I believe I know about mice. To thwart a mouse you must place all desirable mouse food in a sack and hang it high. If you stay in the same place two nights in a row be wary. Your average mouse will have located your stuff the first night. Be cool; be clever; be crafty. Fool him by storing your pack and your food in a new spot the second night. I speak from experience. At Carmanah a mouse chewed through the canvas of

my pack to reach some overlooked trail mix. Trail mix, I've discovered, is very desirable mouse food.

Never underestimate the athletic ability of mice. One evening, at Cribs Creek, after the food was hung, I discovered a partial bag of trail mix still in my pack. Feeling smug, I took the little baggy of nuts and lashed it to a loose rope end near the main food bag. At least six inches separated the two bags as they swung in space. The small bag was so light and unstable, it swayed in the wind. I was confident no reasonable mouse would attempt such a challenge. Wrong! The next morning the hanging baggy had a neatly dissected hole. Only the raisins remained. We may need further study, but I suspect raisins are not desirable mouse food.

53

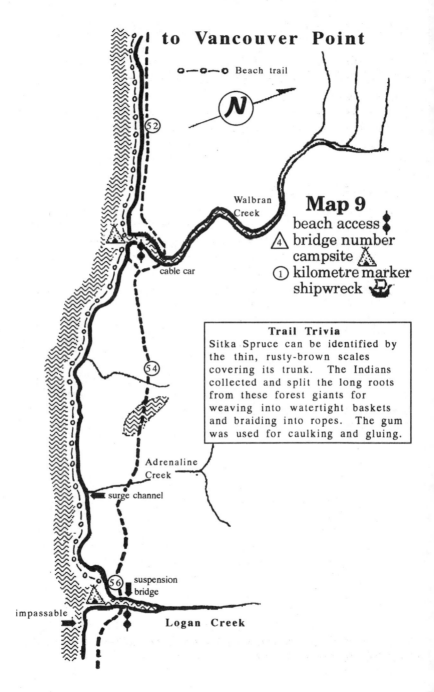

to Vancouver Point

o—o—o Beach trail

N

52

Walbran
Creek

Map 9
beach access
△ 4 bridge number
campsite △
① kilometre marker
shipwreck

cable car

54

Trail Trivia
Sitka Spruce can be identified by
the thin, rusty-brown scales
covering its trunk. The Indians
collected and split the long roots
from these forest giants for
weaving into watertight baskets
and braiding into ropes. The gum
was used for caulking and gluing.

Adrenaline
Creek

← surge channel

56 → suspension
bridge

impassable →

Logan Creek

54

MAP 9: VANCOUVER POINT—LOGAN CREEK

APPROXIMATE TREKKING TIME: 2 1/2 to 3 hours
DISTANCE: 5 KM

This section has it all: steep ladders, endless mud holes and roots, boardwalks over bog, a dangerous surge channel, a cable car, a wonderful sandy beach, a fabulous swimming hole, a spectacular campsite and a heart-thumping bridge over Logan Creek. What a trek!

WALBRAN CREEK

The stretch between Vancouver Point and Walbran Creek is passable by beach when tides are below 3.7 M. An overland route joins the cable car at Walbran to the beach at the north side of Vancouver Point. Walbran itself must be waded when hiking the beach. The water at the mouth is only knee deep during the summer months. It may be much higher during other seasons or when heavy rain has persisted. Take care when crossing.

Walbran Creek campsite is one of the best on the trail. A clear, deep and refreshingly cool (read: ice cold) pond greets weary trekkers. There is plenty of wood for fires and wind shelters.

Of the two routes between Walbran and Logan, the overland route is safer and, for some, quicker. It crosses a swampy area via a series of boardwalks. There are long sections where you are scampering over roots and around mud holes. This ain't no shoppin' mall!

The bog area has some interesting plants, trees and moss. We recommend it for the nature lover and safe trekker alike. Please stay on the boardwalk along this section to preserve the fragile environment and prevent wet feet.

We *do not* recommend taking the beach route. It is mainly over a wide sandstone shelf, broken by tide pools and surge channels. All of this route is passable only when tides are below 2.1 M, except at Adrenaline Creek. *This nasty spot is passable only with tides below 1.7 M.* Keep this in mind when planning your route.

"... Adrenaline Surge..."

ADRENALINE CREEK

The surge channel at Adrenaline Creek is quite likely the most dangerous point on the trail. We have seen many shaken trekkers with skinned knees and soaked packs who did not give this crossing the respect it deserves. People have died here and we cannot over emphasize the need for caution. There is a small waterfall on the south side of the channel that keeps the smooth rocks quite slippery. To compound the misery and danger, you must scurry across this rock face while waves lap at your feet. We have set out from Walbran to try our hand at this section only to discover the water is too high and the cliff very slippery. Miffed, we have had to double back and take the land route. You definitely do not need to add this 1 1/2 hours to your trek.

We suggest that ropes be used in the crossing to provide an extra margin of safety. Hip belts should be unfastened to allow a quick release should you fall in. Our best advice is, give yourself a break and take the inland trail.

Remember, if you have to backtrack, you will require extra time, so watch your tide tables.

LOGAN CREEK

The Logan Creek mouth is wide, but during the summer months the water level is low and the crossing is easy. There are some campsites near the mouth of the creek.

The Logan Creek suspension bridge is a masterpiece of engineering. It offers spectacular, if not heart thumping views from its centre. Access is by steep ladders leading down from either end of the trail, and up from the beach on the south side.

The walls of the creek basin are very steep. Extensive erosion has a nasty habit of knocking trees over the ladders and around the bridge heads. As a result the trail is often hazardous, and the ladders are in less than perfect condition. Watch each step carefully through here.

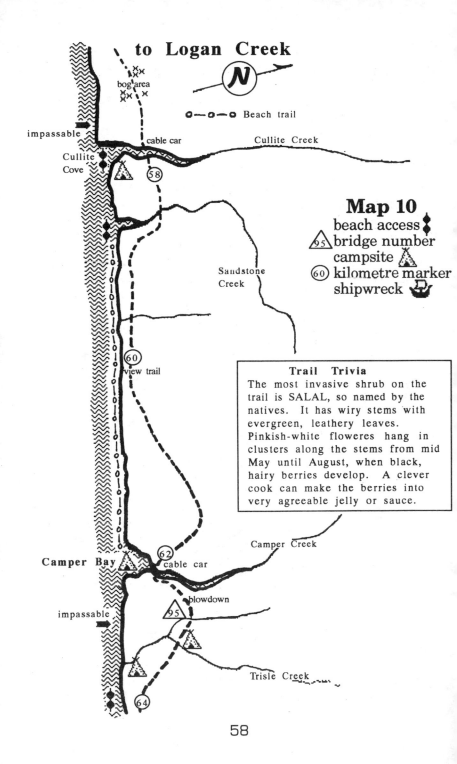

to Logan Creek

N

bog area

Beach trail

impassable

cable car

Cullite Creek

Cullite Cove

58

Map 10
beach access
95 bridge number
campsite
60 kilometre marker
shipwreck

Sandstone Creek

60 view trail

Trail Trivia
The most invasive shrub on the trail is SALAL, so named by the natives. It has wiry stems with evergreen, leathery leaves. Pinkish-white floweres hang in clusters along the stems from mid May until August, when black, hairy berries develop. A clever cook can make the berries into very agreeable jelly or sauce.

62

Camper Bay

cable car

Camper Creek

impassable

95 blowdown

Trisle Creek

64

58

MAP 10: LOGAN CREEK—CAMPER BAY

APPROXIMATE TREKKING TIME: 4 HOURS (BUT CAN
SEEM LIKE DAYS)
DISTANCE: 6 KM

LADDERS

They're HEEEEERE! This section includes some of the most
challenging, frustrating, muddy and generally interesting terrain
along the entire trail. It also has ladders—lots of ladders. Ladders
with over 200 rungs (count them), that never seem to end. We are
talking ladders that climb the equivalent of a 25 to 30 floor building.
Say hello to your cardio-vascular system!

"...ladders that seem to never end..."

Tip:

*Carry a walking stick along this stretch to help keep your
balance as you prance around the mud holes.*

This section requires particular attention. Even if it is not raining, the trail can become a quagmire in places, so step with care and be prepared for frequent mud baths. It's great! There's enough mud and goo in this area to coat us all . In a split second you can end up knee deep or more in the stuff. Should you take the plunge, remind yourself that the world's best spas charge big bucks for this sort of skin treatment.

The trail from Logan, which has steep ladders at either end of the bridge, moves through a swampy area with boardwalks and interesting flora. Many of the trees are ancient and stunted "bonsai" cousins of giant cedars, spruce and hemlock.

CULLITE CREEK

Big ladders greet you at the cable car on Cullite Creek. If you are coming from either direction, you already know what to expect. Sandstone and Logan both have their fair share of ladders, but those at Cullite are the highest of all.

There is a campsite at Cullite Cove, which is bordered by impassable headlands. You have to go down the creek bed from the trail to get to it.

Get your cameras out, the folks back at the office are not going to believe this part of your story.

SANDSTONE CREEK

At Sandstone, as with Cullite, the ladders seem unending, particularly if you are going up. A bridge across this beautiful creek offers a welcome respite before tackling the ladders on the other side. Once you complete this section of the trail, there will be no beanstalk you cannot scale.

The trail between Sandstone and Camper Bay is a maze of giant roots, mini-bogs and fallen logs. It is easiest near the south end, but drops and climbs sharply at Camper.

The beach route between Sandstone and Camper Creek is accessed either from the main trail via the creek bed at Sandstone, or by heading north at Camper Bay.

First the good news: the shelf makes for easy hiking most, but not all the way. There are excellent tidal pools near the south end. Trekking is relatively easy. *Now the bad news:* there is a nasty surge channel near Camper Bay that needs your respect. There is a steep rock at the mouth of Sandstone Creek that will test your mettle whether you are climbing up or sliding down the shelf. It is most difficult when you are heading south.

This rock is easy to recognize because it has about six square yards of skin from the backs of our legs that was left behind when we slid down its rough surface. There is no real trail from the mouth of Sandstone Creek to the bridge. You have to bushwhack your way for about 500 M over logs, rocks and branches. Only use this route late in the season when the water is low.

Tides must be below 1.2 M to get on and off the shelf and across surge channels. The actual shelf between Sandstone and Camper is passable when tides are below 1.7 M. If you decide to take the shelf route, look for a rope hanging down near KM 59. This is another access point you can use if you get into trouble.

There is a mediocre campsite at the mouth of Sandstone. It is suitable only if you find yourself stuck between tides (which, of course, you would never do).

CAMPER BAY

Camper Bay offers excellent, well-protected campsites. There is usually plenty of firewood at the head of the bay, but you may have do some fancy stone-stepping to cross the creek. The creek bed at Camper changes its course every year and sometimes disappears under the gravel before reaching the ocean. Be wary of the tides when you pitch your tent. The creek bed may look innocent but it floods with the rising tide. We have heard wild blasphemy from trekkers who had snuggled down for the night only to find themselves deep in the brine before their time. Look for the high tide line and stay above it.

Tip:
When the tide is rising, you have to go well upstream to get fresh drinking water.

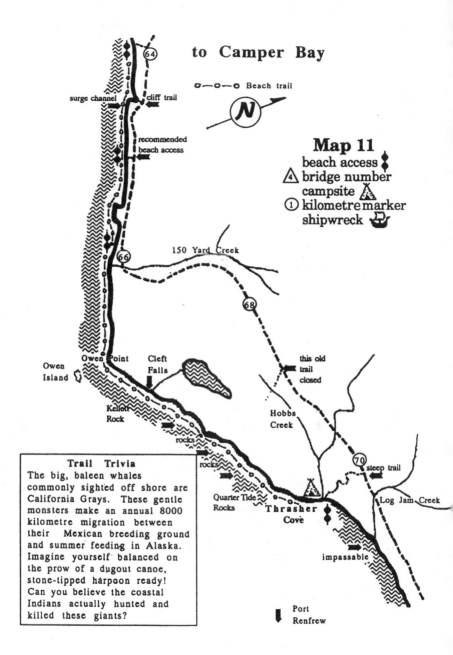

to Camper Bay

⊙—⊙—⊙ Beach trail

N

Map 11
beach access
bridge number ④
campsite 🛆
kilometre marker ①
shipwreck 🛥

64

surge channel   cliff trail

recommended beach access

150 Yard Creek

66

68

Owen Point   Cleft Falls

Owen Island

this old trail closed

Kellott Rock

Hobbs Creek

rocks

rocks

70   steep trail

Log Jam Creek

Trail Trivia
The big, baleen whales
commonly sighted off shore are
California Grays. These gentle
monsters make an annual 8000
kilometre migration between
their Mexican breeding ground
and summer feeding in Alaska.
Imagine yourself balanced on
the prow of a dugout canoe,
stone-tipped harpoon ready!
Can you believe the coastal
Indians actually hunted and
killed these giants?

Quarter Tide Rocks   Thrasher Cove

impassable

Port Renfrew

64

MAP 11: CAMPER BAY—THRASHER COVE

APPROXIMATE TREKKING TIME: 4 HOURS
DISTANCE: 8 KM

There is an option of taking either the beach or the inland trail from Thrasher to KM 64— tides willing. You must take the inland trail between KM 64 and Camper Bay. We strongly recommend that you do not take the KM 64 cut-off (the first one you come to when heading south from Camper and the third beach access point on the shelf north of Owen Point). Instead, we recommend you use the access that is located at approximately KM 65. This is the second beach access marker on the trail when heading south from Camper and the second access marker seen from the shelf north of Owen Point. There is a dangerous surge channel between KM 64 and KM 65 that can ruin your day if you hit it at the wrong time and the tide is high.

The beach section offers a variety of hiking terrains. The inland trail is hidden from the ocean for most of the time. It cuts deep into the woods around Owen Point.

SURGE CHANNEL

The dangerous surge channel between KM 64 and 65 can be crossed when tides are below 1.7 M. If the tide is low enough, a rock will be exposed in the middle of the channel. If necessary, remove your packs and pass them across one at a time. This may not be an easy process but it may save injury.

KM65

Beach access is available at KM 64, 65, and 66. All access points open onto a spectacular shelf that spans the entire section from Owen Point to KM 64. The route is passable if tides are below 2.4 M, however, note that Owen Point may only be rounded when tide levels are below 1.8 M.

The beach access at KM 64 is steep and tricky and should be used by confident, experienced trekkers only. Once again, we strongly urge you to take the access trail at KM 65 because of its relative safety. The shelf south of KM 65 provides an excellent trekking highway. Be careful of lesser surge channels, sandstone caves and other natural barriers found along the way.

OWEN POINT

There is a spectacular cave that you can walk through to get around Owen Point, provided the tide is below 1.8 M. If the tide is rising and you find yourself at Owen Point, you may be able to climb over the point, rather than take the cave route. Look for the ropes at either side.

Look for the sea lions off Owen Point. They can help kill some time if the tides hold you up.

It is important to check tide tables any time you hike the beaches, but it is particularly important for this stretch. The tides must be lower than 2.4 M to get from Thrasher to KM 65, but remember that they must be below 1.8 M to get around Owen Point.

The lower the tide, the easier it will be trekking the stretch from Thrasher to Owen Point. The beach is littered with huge criss-crossing logs and enormous boulders. This route may frequently seem impassable, but if the tides are right, and you watch your step, it is a great route to take.

The inland passage is a marvelous forest walk. Unfortunately, there are no ocean views for the entire distance from Thrasher through to Camper Bay.

Keep in mind that the beach is more interesting. It is also more challenging and you have tides to contend with. The inland trail starts with an aerobic workout, climbing over 500 ft. above Thrasher, and then settles down to a long, beautiful inland trek.

THRASHER COVE

Thrasher Cove is always a welcome sight. For many years, it was a finishing and starting place for hikers, but in 1998 it ceased to be an access point. There are a few good campsites, freshwater and lots of firewood. If you come off the trail, there are a series of very steep switchbacks and ladders that will drop you fifty stories as fast as an elevator.

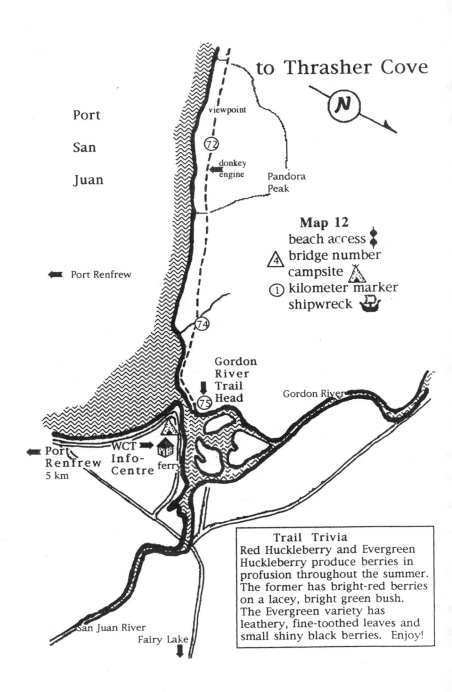

to Thrasher Cove

Port

San

Juan

viewpoint

72

donkey
engine

Pandora
Peak

Map 12
beach access
bridge number
4
campsite
1 kilometer marker
shipwreck

Port Renfrew

74

Gordon
River
Trail
Head

Gordon River

75

Port
Renfrew
5 km

WCT
Info-
Centre   ferry

San Juan River
Fairy Lake

Trail Trivia
Red Huckleberry and Evergreen
Huckleberry produce berries in
profusion throughout the summer.
The former has bright-red berries
on a lacey, bright green bush.
The Evergreen variety has
leathery, fine-toothed leaves and
small shiny black berries. Enjoy!

MAP 12: THRASHER COVE - GORDON RIVER
THE END AND THE BEGINNING

APPROXIMATE TREKKING TIME: 3 1/2 - 4 1/2 HOURS
DISTANCE: 6 KM

This section is all inland. No beach travel is possible.

THRASHER COVE

The trail starts approximately 150 M above the beach at Thrasher Cove. Access to the trail is by a series of steep ladders and switch backs.

The trail is well maintained over the entire distance, but a few gullies are bridged with narrow logs. These logs will test the traction of your boot soles. Move with care.

Visibility is limited along here, but on clear days the lookout at KM 72 provides awesome views of Port San Juan and beyond. There is a campsite near this point, the highest of the entire trail at 230 M. You must climb down to the creek to get water.

A huge, old donkey engine sits by the trail side. We have often wondered at the effort it must have taken for the early loggers to get that machine up there. Hundreds of metres of heavy cable, used decades ago to haul logs to the water, are still stretched taut along the trail.

If you are starting at Gordon River, you should be prepared for an exhausting beginning to your trek. As one friend put it: "Our packs were the heaviest they would be for the entire seven days; our feet were unused to new boots and we had yet to get into the rhythm of the trail. I thought I had started a four hour walk into hell!"

69

So much for bliss! This section has some of the most physically demanding terrain on the whole trail. If you are starting out this is bound to affect you more than if you are ending up. Recognize this beforehand. Your enjoyment of the journey depends as much on your positive mindset as on your physical conditioning. It bothers us to hear people say, 'We had no idea it was so tough!' Take your time! It does get easier. Eventually your pack will become lighter.

GORDON RIVER ACCESS

If you are coming off the trail, the ferry operator will make pick ups four times a day. On your way to the Port Renfrew Hotel, or to the road back to Victoria, make sure you sign out at the Hiker Reception Centre. They would like your comments on trail conditions.

If you are just starting out, you must sign in, get your permit, tide tables and any last minute instructions. If you are finishing, you will have the trek of a life time behind you now, and we hope it was as much fun for you as it has been for us. Let's talk about it sometime over cowboy coffee at Carmanah.

We would also love getting your letters about the trek. You can write to us c/o the publishers, or email us at **wtaitken@home.com.**

SAFE TREKS

The West Coast Trail, in spite of its ruggedness and beauty, can also be hazardous to your health. Most of the time you will have a choice in the matter. Practice safe treks and you can reduce the risk even further. Occasionally, however, matters may be beyond your control. You should be prepared as best you can.

There are about 70 medical evacuations required each year. Most of them relate to sprains, strains and muscle pulls. Wet, slippery conditions, inadequate footwear, poor physical condition, fatigue and excessively heavy packs contributed to these people's downfall. Beware and prepare.

If you have an emergency where outside assistance is needed, here are some of the people who can help:

• Park Wardens (they coordinate and participate in most search and rescue operations, and perform most of the evacuations)
• Trailhead information centre employees
• Quu'as West Coast Trail Group
• Pacheena and Carmanah lightstation keepers
• Nitinat Narrows ferry operators
• Fishermen off the shelves between Camper Bay and Owen Point
• Coast Guard helicopters
• other hikers (don't be shy if you really need help)

The Quu'as West Coast Trail Group provides a staff of six Trail Guardians to patrol throughout the hiking season. The three First Nations groups (Pacheedaht, Ditidaht and Huu-ah-aht) that have reserve lands along the trail, provide this necessary service.

HYPOTHERMIA

Hypothermia accounts for nearly 1 in 10 medical evacuations. It can be fatal if not treated as a life-threatening emergency. It can also be prevented.

Hypothermia results from the body's core temperature dropping to a point where it cannot generate heat on its own.

Uncontrolled shivering is a red flag that hypothermia may be on its way.

If this happens, find shelter, build a fire and work hard to dry out and get warm. If the core temperature drops another degree or two, the victim will become lethargic. The muscles which have been shivering to generate heat will stop doing so. The quality of the victim's voice may change. When this happens, there may be a major emergency at hand. Immediate action must be taken to restore body heat. Simply wrapping the person in a sleeping bog is not enough. Remember they are not generating heat on their own. If possible, strip the victim and place them in a sleeping bag that has been heated over a fire. Another person, who is also stripped, may have to join the victim as another important source of heat. Do not rub the victim's skin or give them anything to drink when they are in his condition. In cases of extreme hypothermia, try to locate a Park Warden to coordinate an evacuation. Once the person's temperature increases, a high calorie meal will assist recovery.

Remember: hypothermia can be prevented. We have seen school kids and adults wearing garbage bags in the pouring rain. Better than nothing, but risky. Proper rain gear is essential. Remember to cover your head, as most of your heat loss is through your noggin.

SUN AND HEAT EXPOSURE

If you are lucky, you will be exposed to the sun for extended periods of time. The reflection off the water intensifies the sun's impact, so take care to protect exposed areas of the skin.   Bring a hat!   Overheating usually happens to a person who is not accustomed to the heat or vigorous exercise.

Victims of heat exertion may became dizzy, suddenly tired, or faint. The best treatment is to rest, cool off and drink extra fluids.

Prevention of heat exertion and more severe heat exhaustion is easy.   When you are exercising strenuously in hot weother, you must make a conscious effort to drink LOTS of fluids. For an average person in very hot weather, that may mean drinking four or five litres of fluid a day. **Remember to filter or treat all water.**

FIRST AID KITS

Every trekker should carry a first aid kit.   It does not have to be expensive, in fact, the home grown variety may be cheaper and better.   Whichever you choose, do not forget to have it handy in your pack.

Suggested items include:
- Moleskin, or second skin, etc. (for blisters)
- Band-Aids - wide assortment
- Small folding scissors
- Mercurochrome or iodine
- Aspirin (also helps keep swelling down)
- Sunscreen (at least #15)
- Needle tweezers (slivers abound)
- Nail clippers (cut them short before you start)

A lot of this stuff can be found on good old Swiss Army Knives.

TIDE TABLES

Beach routes are often restricted in their use due to high tide levels. Anyone who has experienced the frustration of having to backtrack because of rising tides, or felt the fear of being trapped between steep cliffs and the deep blue sea, will vouch for the value of tide tables.

Tide tables are available free of change at the Parks Canada Information Offices, located near each trailhead. The tables are for Tofino (a village located on the west coast of Vancouver Island) and one hour must added to the times stated, to adjust for daylight saving time.

*The example shown in this section is for a **fictional** month of July.* The table covers a four day period from Thursday July 7th to Sunday 10th. Heights of the tides are shown in feet and metres at their highest and lowest points during the day, as recorded on a 24 hour clock.

EXAMPLE 1:

If you wanted to take the beach route from Thrasher Cove to Owen Point, which is passabie at tides below 2.4 M, on Saturday the 9th, you could do so, starting from 1030 (0930, plus one hour).

Day	Time	Ht/Ft	Ht/M
	TIDE TABLE - *EXAMPLE ONLY*		
Tofino-July	DO NOT USE THIS EXAMPLE ON THE TRAIL		

Day	Time	Ht/Ft	Ht/M
7	0050	3.1	.9
TH	0645	8.5	2.6
	1230	4.3	1.3
	1900	10.9	3.3
8	0155	2.6	.8
FR	0810	8.4	2.6
	1335	5.0	1.5
	1955	10.9	3.3
9	0300	2.2	.7
SA	0930	8.5	2.6
	1440	5.5	1.7
	2050	10.9	3.3
10	0400	1.8	.5
SU	1035	8.8	2.7
	1545	5.7	1.7
	2145	11.0	3.4

EXAMPLE 2:

The beach route between Darling and Tsocowis Creek is passable when tides are below 3.7 M. During July there are no tides above 3.4 M, therefore it is safe to trek this section at any time.

EXAMPLE 3:

The surge channel at Adrenaline Creek (known as Adrenaline Surge) is passable at tides below 1.7M. On Saturday the 9th, the tide will be at this height at 1540 (1440, plus one hour) and will not go below this depth during the rest of the day. The only time on the 9th that you can go through this dangerous section would be from 0400 to approximately 0700, when the incoming tide is still less than 1.7 M. We told you to take the trail!

75

EQUIPMENT

The equipment used on the trail is as varied as the personalities and experience of the trekkers who carry it. We have seen people

carrying giant salad bowls, video cameras, and multi-burner stoves. Sleeping bags as big as mattresses and ghetto blasters with giant speakers have all found their way to the trail.   At Carmanah, we met one fellow who had all his world belongings on his back.   He expected the West Coast Trail to be a road!

Equipment planning breaks down to two choices: blisters or bliss. We prefer bliss.

Unless you have hired Sherpas, your pack weight should not exceed 25 - 30% of your body weight. Therefore, a 120 lb. person should not try to carry more than 30 - 35 lb. A person weighing 180 lb. should draw the line between 45 - 55 lb. unless you plan on beating the heck out of yourself!

Here is what we consider to be mandatory equipment:

Rain Gear

The weather along the West Coast Trail is apt to change from fine to foul with little notice. A waterproof pack cover, jacket and pants are mandatory.

Many hikers consider a poncho to be an excellent means of protection. They keep most of the rain out, are comparatively inexpensive and pack well. They are also bulky to wear and likely to have areas open up to the elements at inopportune times.

"Gore-Tex" types of materials -- those that are water resistant but allow moisture out -- are very popular. They are also much more expensive than ponchos or nylon fabric counter-parts. Remember that even these high-tech fabrics are not totally waterproof and can "fail" if you are exposed to rain for too long.

Nylon is a great wind breaker but does not "breathe" well. It works well if you're standing still, but if you are hiking your own sweat will soak you from the inside out. It may be cheaper and pack better than the high tech fabrics, but it creates sauna conditions when you are working hard.

Boots

Boots are perhaps the most important equipment in your arsenal. Your boots may become your best friend or your dreaded enemy. Choose well, you will be looking at them a lot. The key to good boots is that they must feel comfortable. Yes, there will be a "breaking in" period after you first buy them. Yes, they will feel better, to a point, the longer you wear them; but DO NOT LEAVE THE STORE UNLESS THEY ARE COMFORTABLE TO BEGIN WITH. If the clerk tells you that they have to be broken in before they feel good, run—do not walk—from the store.

77

Boots should be comfortable, lightweight (no full steel shanks) and highly water resistant. Ensure your heel is held snugly in place. Blisters are guaranteed if your heel rides up the back of your boot, or if your toes are allowed to jam into the ends. Feel the inside of the boot to determine the quality of the finished seams—rough seams equal blisters, smooth seams equal bliss. Soles should be designed with excellent grips (such as Vibran-type soles) and attached to the boot with waterproof seals. A nice touch is for the tongues to be sown to the sides of the uppers to help keep the elements from leaking in. Firm ankle support is also important, so do not try to do this trail with running shoes. When you are up to your knees in mud around Logan, or climbing the ladders at Sandstone, you will be glad you selected your boots wisely.

Tents

Not everyone hikes with a tent. Some use tarps, one-person bivys, or army-issued hoochies. We use a tent with a water-proof fly and strongly recommend that others do too. Whatever you prefer, keep it light and rain-proof. Even when it's not raining, the humidity can increase significantly during the night and fog is frequently part of the scene.

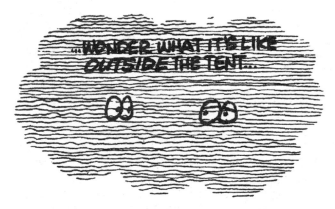

Always allow for as much air to circulate inside your tent as possible. We have seen people cover their tents with plastic, or close all their vents when they hit the sack. It's a wonder they survived the night. Maybe they packed oxygen tanks.

Stoves

A single burner will serve you well. There are lots of very good styles, but, we use a Coleman Peak 1 with a 1/3 litre tank. A one litre Sigg aluminum bottle, plus the tank will provide enough fuel for two people if you use it sparingly (no roasting 20 lb. turkeys). Add another bottle for every two people. Purists may scoff at using stoves. We have been glad to have them on many rainy occasions and they are environmentally friendly.

Packs

When you are not thinking about your feet, chances are your pack will have captured your attention. External frame packs used to be seen more frequently than the internal frame variety, probably because they are available in a lower price range. While we have not completed a thesis study on this subject, it appears that internal frame packs are more popular these days. Both styles offer lots of outside pockets and access options. Even if there are no outside pockets, you can usually secure whatever you want to your pack with bungies, rope, bootlaces, and just about anything else that you can tie in  a knot. There is no great mystery about what type of pack to buy provided you get one that is comfortable. Your pack should have good hip and shoulder straps that are adjustable when you walk. Most of the weight of the pack should be on your hips, so it is most important that the belt is comfortable. The pack adjustment motion, or 'West Coast Trail Boogie", will be keeping you busy if your pack does not fit properly. Make sure your salesperson helps you adjust your new pack, before you leave the store.

Sleeping Bags

Weight is a key factor to consider when choosing a sleeping bag. Any experienced backpacker knows that every ounce saved adds points to the bliss factor.

A three season bag, which is practical for temperatures down to 0°C is quite satisfactory. You can always wear your longjohns and socks to bed if you find the chill too much. Synthetic fibres and down bags offer the best warmth/weight ratio. Synthetic bags are less expensive than their down-filled counter parts.

They are preferred for this reason and the fact that they will dry out faster if they become wet. Both types offer excellent comfort within their temperature limits.

Your bag should be carried in a waterproof stuff sack at all times. In addition, we wrap our sleeping bags inside large, plastic garbage bags for added security. At night we put our packs, boots and other miscellaneous gear into the plastic bag to keep critters and humidity out.

Other Equipment Considerations

- This book
- Sharp hatchet (Dave insists, Wayne feels it's optional)
- Sleeping pad (Therm-a-rests are divine, foam will do)
- Cooking pot (2-3 litre), lid is optional
- Table spoon (no need of forks, table knives)
- Water bottle
- Matches and/or bic lighter
- Fire starter sticks or cubes
- First aid kit
- 30-50 feet of nylon rope
- Biodegradable soap (use sand for cleaning dishes)
- Toilet tissue (one full roll per person)

- Warm pants (avoid jeans and other cottons because they
  soak up water)
- Flashlight (with fresh batteries)
- Wool or polypropylene socks
- Lightweight longjohns
- Hat
- Gloves
- Warm wool or polypropylene sweater or sweat shirt
- Pile jackets (great if you can fit them in)
- Running shoes or Tevas (for camp, NOT the trail)
- Nylon waterproof stuff bags (lots)
- Plastic garbage bags (don't forget the ties)

FOOD FOR THOUGHT

We have yet to meet a trekker who, at some time during the trip, did not have their thoughts focused solely on food. The cravings start the first day and build to an obsession by trail's end. The Port Renfrew and Bamfield docks have seated many a blister-footed trekker inhaling cheeseburgers, cold pop and french fries. Some people trek and eat others eat to trek, but we trek to eat.

Meal time is a special part of the trip for us. The tent is up, the fire is burning nicely on the beach, and our stomachs are reminding us to get on with it. We stretch meal time out for as long as we can, restricted only by the degree of our appetites, weight of our food and creativity of the chef.

Your body will be burning twice as many calories on a trek like this, so it is important to plan your menu carefully. Once you start the trail, there is nothing in the way of food supplies for over 75 km. We have seen people who have been out of supplies with more than a day remaining. This situation could have been prevented with better planning.

Packaging is also important. We still wonder if the bulging plastic bag of pork and beans that one hiker had swinging recklessly from the back of his pack, ever made it to the pot. We wonder too, if the heavy cans of ham and chicken that another had stuffed into her sleeping bag justified the effort needed to haul them up the ladders at Cullite.

Tips:

Hiking the West Coast Trail fosters hearty appetites. We offer the following tips and recipes in good taste:

• Double bag everything. Bag it again in another bag and bag it some more. Take along some extra bags. Rain, heavy dew and unscheduled falls into tidal pools can drench your food supplies and make your trip miserable. Extra bagging will also help prevent spills and leakage into the nether parts of your pack.

• Buy the highest quality food you can afford. Foods containing little or no additives provide a nutritional advantage. Pasta is very versatile, nutritious and an excellent source of carbohydrates. Instead of spaghetti noodles, which are very sharp, try pasta shells. Shells also pack better than bulky macaroni.

• Beginning a meal with hot soup provides a quick, refreshing and easy way to take the edge off your appetite. Your body will be grateful for the fluids. "Mayacamas" brand debydrated soups are generally excellent. For a hearty meal you can throw in some instant rice and dried peas.

• Japanese ramen soups are light, well packaged and easy to prepare. If you want the taste kicked up a notch or two, try adding a pinch of curry and a teaspoon of crushed chilies. Hang around to enjoy the contorted expressions that follow the first mouthful.

• Garlic, onions and carrots are well worth their bulk and weight since they add a nutritious, tasty touch to your meals. Pack these in a paper bag, or in a manner that allows them to breathe. They will keep longer and you can use the bag as fire starter.

• Keep fuel and stoves separate from the pack that contains the food, unless you like petroleum flavoured fettucini. If you must carry them in the same pack, place the fuel containers lower than the food.

• Hang all your food up at night. The West Coast Trail varmints have been bred to sniff out a package of triple-bagged trail mix at a range of 3 KM. and they can chew through any pack to get it. Dave's pack looks like a patchwork quilt, yet he is still amazed each time he discovers these critters have gnawed yet another hole to get at their dinner.

EPICUREAN DELIGHTS

Some recipes were created to bring joy and happiness to any trekker. Here are a few we have tried and recommend.

Sam's Garlic Pasta

• 3 cups of pasta
• 1 bulb (not clove) garlic - chopped
• 1 medium onion - diced
• 1/4 cup olive oil
• 1 handful parmesan cheese
• 2 tbs. crushed red chilies

Boil pasta until tender.

Sauce: Heat olive oil, saute garlic and crushed chilies. Do not brown the garlic as it will become bitter. Add the sauce to the pasta (do not remove the garlic) and mix in the parmesan cheese. Serve with plenty of water.
Note: you can add more garlic, at your partner's risk.

Wayne's Glayva Pancakes

• 2 cups pancake mix
• 3 tbs. margarine or butter
• 12 oz. pure maple syrup
• 4 oz. Glayva (a scotch-based liqueur that looks remarkably like maple syrup)
• Berries if you've got them and know them
• 2 cups water

Mix pancake ingredients and water to form batter. Add the berries. Add batter to heated frying pan. Check the temperature of the pan first by adding a drop of water—it should sizzle and bounce around a bit.

Reach for the maple syrup but pick up the Glayva by mistake and add 4 oz. to your pancake.

Try to act like you knew what you were doing.

Cowboy Coffee

- 2/3 cup ground coffee (the real stuff)
- 4 to 5 cups of water
- 3 tbs. honey
- 1/2 cup milk

Boil water in a pan and add coffee. Simmer. Add honey and stir until dissolved.

Add milk slowly, stir again and continue to simmer for another 5 minutes. Serve very hot.

Tip:
> *Real cowboys may not use honey.*

Tip:
> *Scratch a line on your mug at the one cup mark. This is handy for measuring and essential for making sure your hiking companions don't get more than their fair share of the goodies.*

David's Lip Welding Pasta

- 3 cups pasta
- 1 package Mayacamas Tomato Soup Mix
- 455 ml hot salsa (heavy, but worth its weight)
- 1 oz. olive oil
- dash salt
- 1 handful parmesan cheese
- 3 pita bread

Bring 6 cups of water to a boil and add the oil and salt. Cook pasta until tender.

Sauce: Prepare tomato soup mix using the sauce instructions. Add salsa and heat.

Serve over pasta, add parmesan cheese. Wipe the bottom of the plate with pita bread to get all the sauce.

Roy's Masterpiece

The following meal was prepared for us by a long time trekking partner. Yes, he carries a blue pin-striped backpack.

Trekker Bonding Time

- black olives
- melba toast
- bonding lotion

Add oysters and olives to melba toast, wash down with bonding lotion

The Soup SVP

- French onion soup (from mix)
- croutons (from New York Pizza Bagel Chips)
- Parmesan cheese

prepare soup, add croutons, cover with Parmesan cheese

Entree (Linguine Pesto Rosa)

- basic tomato, basil Parmesan, cheese sauce (from Knorr)
- spinach linguine
- dried elephant ear mushrooms
- freeze dried tomatoes
- baby clams (can)
- baby shrimp (another can)
- 1 bulb garlic
- 2 oz. olive or canola oil

Rehydrate mushrooms and tomatoes. Prepare pasta sauce per instructions on the package. Saute garlic and add with clams, shrimp mushrooms and tomatoes to the pasta. Add Parmesan cheese to taste.

We recommend this menu under the following conditions:

-There are no other trekkers around to laugh at you.
-You have a red and white checked table cloth.
-Your chef likes to carry cans (full and empty) for a week.

FOOD STUFF

Here are some of the food items we have taken along over the years.

- coffee, tea (herbal and high test)
- powdered milk
- soya sauce (from your last Chinese meal)
- margarine (butter goes rancid)

- garlic (one of the four major food groups)
- onions
- carrots
- lentils

- carob or chocolate bars
- popping corn (it drives other trekkers mad—bring lots)
- trail mix (add lots of M & M's)
- licorice

- Japanese-style ramen soup or Mayacamas soups and sauces
- Taste Adventure Black Bean Chili, or Pinto Beans
- Magic Pantry packaged dinners—heavy but tasty
- Natural High dehydrated meals
- any kind of dehydrated vegetables

- rice
- pasta (all kinds but spaghetti can be sharp so watch it)
- instant pancake mix, granola cereal, instant porridge, etc.
- soy burger mix

- olive or canola oil
- brown sugar
- cinnamon

- garlic powder, onion powder, curry powder
- crushed chilies, chili flakes, salsa, etc.
- cheese - parmesan, cheddar, gouda, creamed, etc.
- peanut or almond butter crackers—all kinds—lots of uses
- sardines, tuna, salmon, oysters, shrimp, etc.
- dried sausage, pepperoni, jerky, etc.
- pita bread, bagels, etc.
- cookies (make sure they pack well)

FOR WHATEVER IT'S WORTH DEPARTMENT

At the beginning of our book, we stated a goal of providing information which would be useful for both the seasoned trekker and the novice. The following tips are offered to all of you, for whatever they are worth.

• Place your feet above your hips when resting on the trail. Your legs will relax faster and you and your toes will become friends again.

• Pack each meal in separate plastic bags, then pack each day's meals in a common bag and label it. This method provides quick access to your food and reduces the chances of breakage due to handling.

• Old film containers make excellent spice containers.

• Scrub your pots and pans with sand and ocean water. It is abundant, cheap, effective and will not pollute.

• Place a cap from an aerosol can in the bottom of your tent pole bag. The poles won't tear the fabric.

• Take care that your tent poles do not become plugged with sand. Partially plugged connections can cause pole tips to break.

• At the end of the day's trek, set up your shelter first. The weather can change very quickly.

• As soon as you get into camp, strip off damp clothes and replace them with dry layers to suit the temperature. This will prevent chills, and in extreme cases the onset of hypothermia.

• Tie a damp bandanna loosely around your neck on hot days. It will act as a radiator to keep you and your photos looking cool.

• Hike at a pace comfortable for the slowest trekker in your group. This will keep you in sight of each other and help ensure everyone arrives safely with energy to spare.

•Pack the heaviest items high and close to your back. This will keep the centre of gravity as normal as possible and assist in your balance when trekking.

• Keep sharp items away from the sides of your pack. It takes very little movement to wear a hole in the material, or in your back.

• Pack stoves and fuel in plastic bags to keep spills and fumes contained. Stoves often have nasty edges so cover them well.

• Leave glass containers at home. They are heavy, fragile and a source of pollution.

• Put peanut butter on a squeaky pack connection. It is a good lubricant and may help save your sanity. Be careful to keep your pack out of the way of critters who may be drawn to the smell.

• Keep tent flaps open as wide as possible at night. The fresh air feels great, and the condensation on the inside of your tent walls will be reduced.

Tips: (continued)

• Treat blisters with moleskin, or second skin-type products at the first sign of irritation. The added padding on "hot spots" will help prevent a painful situation from getting further out of hand.

• Save your hiking for daylight hours. It is not worth the risk to try and make tide deadlines in the dark.

• Leave dogs at home. They are not allowed on the West Coast Trail.

• An extra set of boot laces take up little room and will serve as a clothesline, pack/tent repair kit, bedroll straps, etc. Who knows, you might even need them to tie up your boots!

• Undo hip and chest belts when crossing surge channels and fast moving streams. This will allow for a quick release should you fall.

Tips: (continued)

• Treat all drinking water by filtering, boiling or iodine.

• Keep your tent well away from creeks and streams. The closer they are, the greater amount of humidity and noise. More importantly, many of them flood with the tides or sudden rain showers that frequent the area.

• Keep pack weights well under 30% of your body weight. If you must carry more than this, hire Sherpas so you can enjoy the trip.

• Pita bread and bagels pack well and keep for days. Watch out for crows and varmints, since they like these foods as much as trekkers do.

• Bring a pair of running shoes or Tevas to wear around the campsite. The comfort they bring is worth their weight in Treasury Bills.

• Cut the feet off an old pair of long wool socks and recycle the tubes as gaiters to keep out those beach stones.

• Bring along a bladder from a wine or apple juice box. You can keep several litres of water at your campsite and it collapses into a handful when you pack up.

• On windy and/or rainy days, dig a small pit in the sand to build your fire. There will be more protection from the elements this way, and you may warm up faster.

TRAVEL CONNECTIONS (all area codes are 250)

Air Lines

Air Canada.. 360-9074
Air BC... 360-9074
Canadian Airlines... 382-6111
Lake Union Air (Seattle) 1-800-826-1890
Horizon Air (Washington, Oregon) 1-800-547-9308
WestJet (Alberta, Saskatchewan) 1-800-538-5696

Pacific Spirit Air (coastal charters) 537-9359
Harbour Air Seaplanes (Vancouver-Victoria) 1-800-665-0212

Ferries

BC Ferry Information.. 386-3431
Washington State Ferries (Sidney-Anacortes) 656-1531
Black Ball (MV Coho, Victoria-Port Angeles).................. 386-2202

Victoria Clipper (Victoria-Seattle) 382-8100
Alberni Marine Transportation.......... 723-8313 or 1-800-663-7192
                    (the Lady Rose, Bamfield-Port Alberni)
Nitinat Lake Water-Taxi .... 745-3509 or 745-8124
                    (leaving at mid-trail)
Butch Jack Hiker Ferry Service.. 647-5517
                    (Gordon River Trailhead)

Public Transportation

Pacific Coach Lines (Up Island/Victoria - BC Ferries) 385-4411

Metro Transit (Greater Victoria buses) 382-6161

West Coast Trail Express 477-8700
                    (Victoria - Port Renfrew & Bamfield)
Western Bus Lines.. 723-3341
                    (Port Alberni - Bamfield)
Pacheenaht First Nation's Bus.. 647-5521
                    (Port Renfrew - Nitinat- Bamfield)

Other Useful Contacts

Pacific Rim National Park (trail & general park information) ...726-7721
Quu'as West Coast Trail Group...................................... 723-4393
CNCP Telecommunications.. 384-7174
Tourism BC... 387-1642
Tourism Victoria... 382-2127
Youth Hostel Victoria.. 385-4511
Pachena Bay WCT Hiker Registration Office
.... Phone / Fax 728-3234
Gordon River WCT Hiker Registration Office
.... Phone / Fax 647-5434

Web Sites

• Tips 'n Tales of the West Coast Trail
http://www.islandnet.com/~davfoste/
   The official site of Blisters and Bliss. A collection of the stories behind many of
the cartoons.

• A West Coast Trail hike at a glance- By Karen Sykes
http://www.seattle-pi.com/pi/getaways/071797/days17.html
   A concise, six day itinerary worth looking at.

• The West Coast Trail - Where we started
http://www.islandnet.com/~friesen/trail1.htm
   An informative general description.

• A photo collection
http://www.sookenet.com/sooke/activity/trails/views.html
   Need some pictures to inspire you?

• A preparation guide produced by the Pacific Rim National Park
Reserve & Quu'as West Coast Trail Group
http://sookenet.com/activity/trails/wctguide.html
   Essential reading for all hikers. Printed copies are available at the trailheads.

• On the West Coast Trail: A Personal Perspective by Ray
Siemens
http://purl.oclc.org/NET/FullStride.html
   An entertaining account of what hiking the WCT is often like.

• The West Coast Trail by Warren Long
http://members.home.net/warren2.long/Hiking/wct.html
   This is undoubtedly the most comprehensive account of a one week journey
along the West Coast Trail. The pictures are awesome.

COMFORT INSURANCE
An extra light-weight tarp
always earns its keep!

Use it above your tent in heavy rain. Sleep
under it during clear skies.

When rain persists, rig your fly up
high for cooking or lounging.

Block wind by erecting a vertical barrier.

Lucky you! Sip your drink in the
shade of your tarp.

In cold weather, a tarp behind a
fire will reflect the heat.

95

TURNING ON THE HEAT

Want to change your campy body odor with some powerful, tenacious smoke smells? Here's your chance! The West Coast Trail usually has fuel in abundance and ideal surroundings for enjoying a fire. While we use a stove for most of our cooking, there are certain times when only real fire can create the true trekking experience. Coffee is big on our list! Our big, stainless steel pot percolates in the coals through and after the dinner hours, providing the best in cowboy coffee. If you catch a cod, or buy some along the way, we think campfire cooking is the only way to go.

Need a reason to invite an interesting person over? Build a cozy, beckoning fire.

A simple, keyhole fire is the most common for general use. Keyhole refers to the circle of stones open at one end for drawing out cooking coals or setling in a pot. In wind or rough weather a trench fire will give a more uniform heat for cooking. A base in sand or beach gravel won't need to be lined with stones.

96

Tips:

•In wet weather, dry wood may be found in the lower dead branches of a large tree, or the inside of a cedar log. Put a good piece of dry cedar under cover for the morning kindling.

•Feed long pieces in from one side of the fire and keep pushing them in as they burn.

•In cold weather, a fire on the protected side of a big log will reflect and radiate the heat. Be careful not to set your fire too close to the log. You may find yourself with enough heat to make bronze, but lose your heat radiator.

•Damp or partially rotten wood may help keep a fire smouldering through the night.

•In heavy rain, lean a flat log above the fire to act as a night-time roof.

•Two six inch logs rolled side by side over the hot coals will likely still be smouldering next morning. The chill experienced when you first crawl from the sack will soon be forgotten.

•Carry fire starter cubes or sticks.

•If you bring matches, leave the "water proof" variety at home. They are usually useless. "Strike anywhere" matches, wrapped in baggies and stored in different parts of your pack will serve you better. The most reliable fire starter is a good old Bic lighter. In dry weather, paper matches are fine too.

FIRE FLASHES

Do:

Keep charcoal ash and other remains of your fire in one spot.
Use a previously developed fire pit. Use water for extinguishing.

Don't:

Put your fire out by spreading it around or smothering it with sand.
Build it near trees or roots.
Leave it burning, unattended.
Leave cans, bottles or other garbage behind in the fireplace.
Place it up wind, or too near your tent.

THE TREKKER

LIFE ON THE BEACH
tracking creatures from the intertidal zone

SPLASH ZONE

MIDDLE TIDE ZONE

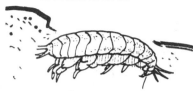

Beach Hoppers rise around your feet as you walk the sand.

Periwinkles seldom go in the water.

Goose Barnacles collect food as they sway in the surf.

Mussels cling to the rocks by the thousands.

Anemones inject poison into their prey but aren't harmful to humans.

Shore Crabs are purple and green and hide under rocks.

Black Turbans live in tide pools.

LIFE ON THE BEACH
tracking creatures from the intertidal zone

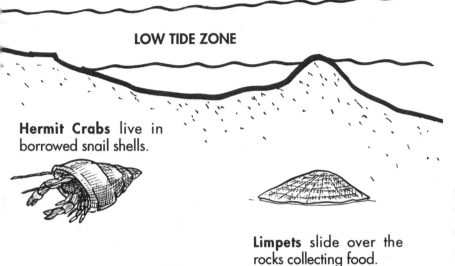

LOW TIDE ZONE

Hermit Crabs live in borrowed snail shells.

Limpets slide over the rocks collecting food.

Black Chitons are protected by overlapping shells.

Tidepool Sculpins, or Bullheads, change their colour to match the surroundings.

101

FIT BITS

We have often been asked by potential trail trekkers if we thought they could handle the 77 KM distance of the West Coost Trail. There is no pat answer. We offer the following comments if you are considering this challenge.

First of all, you must have a positive mind set going into this trip. You can have the strength of Popeye or Olive Oil, but if you are not mentally prepared you will be miserable, you will make others unhappy, and you could get hurt. Bottom line—you have to really want to do this trip!

People have died along this rugged coast. The surge channels are particularly dangerous and the many ladders are not for the faint of heart. Long slippery logs over deep ravines and slimy green stuff at the water's edge are often part of your highway.

There are about 70 emergency evacuations annually for cuts, bruises, exhaustion, fractures and hypothermia. You will have to carry a minimum of 30 lb. for at least four hours per day, if you expect to complete the trek in six days. Your body needs to be conditioned to handle this amount of stress, so a high level of physical fitness is essential.

Some people make the mistake of going on the West Coost Trail to "get in shape". If you are not physically capable of meeting the challenges before you start, the trail is more likely to injure you than make you more fit. No matter what shape you are in, expect to experience tired, sore muscles at day's end. The good news is—bed never feels as good as after a day of slogging it out in the harness.

Sally Larrington, a fitness instructor, world traveler, entrepreneur and trekker extraordinaire has compiled a few exercises to help prepare you for the rigors of the trail They can help keep you from seizing into a fetal position during the trek.

EXERCISES FOR SITTING OR STANDING.
THESE CAN BE DONE ALMOST ANY TIME, WITHOUT WARM-UP.
WATCH YOUR BALANCE IF YOU'RE WEARING YOUR PACK.

Don't do full head rolls (head leaning back)-- just half-circles...

LOOK OVER A SHOULDER, THEN SLOWLY ROLL YOUR HEAD DOWN, GENTLY PRESSING CHIN ON CHEST, THEN LOOK OVER OTHER SHOULDER. REPEAT.

TILT HEAD FROM SIDE TO SIDE, EAR TO EACH SHOULDER.

.. FACE STRAIGHT AHEAD (1.), LOOK DOWN (2.) AND BACK UP 2.STRAIGHT AHEAD (3.), THEN LEFT (4,5) AND RIGHT (6,7). REPEAT.

... PRESS ONE SIDE, THEN OTHER...

RELAX HANDS, ELBOWS, SHOULDERS...

."ROTATE" SHOULDERS: FORWARD, UP, BACK. DO TOGETHER, THEN SEPARATELY. RELAX ARMS.

"SHRUG" ONE SHOULDER; HOLD; RELEASE. THEN OTHER SHOULDER. REPEAT

"SHRUG" BOTH SHOULDERS... HOLD... RELEASE...

SITTING EXERCISES

Breathe deeply & regularly while exercising. Don't hold your breath when exerting yourself...

GENTLY PULL UP TO SIT "TALL" WITH BACK STRAIGHT. HOLD... RELAX. REPEAT.

"CURVE" YOUR BACK AND NECK. HUG KNEES... HOLD... RELEASE. REPEAT.

START, SITTING "ALL...

ROUND BACK AND RECLINE UNTIL LOWER BACK TOUCHES GROUND. HOLD. RETURN TO START.

PUT FINGERTIPS BEHIND EARS -- DON'T TRY TO PULL YOURSELF UP WITH YOUR HANDS.

KEEP KNEES BENT

LIFT & TWIST SHOULDER TOWARDS OPPOSITE KNEE... REPEAT WITH OPPOSITE SHOULDERS/KNEES...

REACH FORWARD & RAISE UPPER BODY. HOLD... THEN RETURN.

YOU SHOULD WARM UP (A MINIMUM OF 15 MINUTES' EASY HIKING) BEFORE DOING THE FOLLOWING. THESE ARE IMPORTANT EXERSISES. YOU DON'T HAVE TO DO ALL EACH TIME; CHOOSE A VARIETY. TRY TO TAKE AT LEAST TWO EXERCISE BREAKS EACH DAY.

CLASP FINGERS, STRETCH UP DIAGONALLY (1) THEN OVER TO SIDE, AND DOWN (2). REPEAT TO OTHER SIDE.

SWING ARMS FORWARD AND BACK, ALTERNATELY

SIT. SLOWLY TWIST TO THIS POSITION... HOLD BRIEFLY, THEN RETURN TO ORIGINAL POSITION. TWIST TO OPPOSITE SIDE ... HOLD ... RETURN. REPEAT.

WHEN DOING ANY STRETCHING EXERCISES, *HOLD EACH STRETCH FOR 10 SECONDS OR SO.*

IMPORTANT: AVOID "BOUNCING" WHEN IN A STRETCH POSITION: DON'T FORCE YOUR BODY TO STRETCH TOO FAR.

 START...

 TWIST...

 PRESS GENTLY... HOL

START WITH STRAIGHT BACK...

.. "ROUND" BACK AND NECK... HOLD... RETURN TO STRAIGHT BACK. REPEAT.

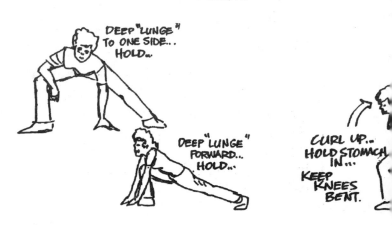

DEEP "LUNGE" TO ONE SIDE... HOLD..

DEEP "LUNGE" FORWARD... HOLD..

CURL UP.. HOLD STOMACH IN... KEEP KNEES BENT.

"LUNGES" ARE SMOOTH, CONTROLLED MOVEMENTS; DON'T "BOUNCE" INTO THEM. HOLD FOR 10+ SECONDS.

KEEP
KNEES
BENT

TOUCH TOE TO GROUND... THEN
HEEL TO GROUND. REPEAT
WITH OTHER FOOT.

FINISH WITH
A COOL-DOWN.
Raise arms
out & up; breathe
in deeply.
Lower arms;
Breathe out.
REPEAT.

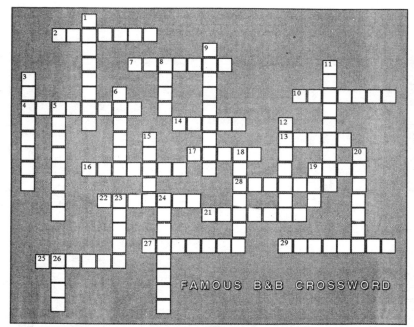

FAMOUS B&B CROSSWORD

ACROSS

2 three short a's
4 boiling is big business here
7 tooo many
10 almost a breakfast cereal
13 dangerous water
14 mix all the colours
16 true love
17 not for babies only
19 truth and ......
21 more than 200 rungs
22 famous foot ailment
25 far south
27 rocky warning
28 more like a lake than a river
29 bovine sighting

DOWN

1 ship that built the trail
3 a town divided by water
5 river of urine
6 trekker with a tent
8 rocks unlimited
9 possible full name of boy named Sue
11 Troll's favourite sighting
12 water falling down
15 feet up, drink in hand
18 triangular marker
19 paternal cookie maker
20 leave out the port
23 suspended in space
24 many trekkers end and start here
26 common WCT four-letter utterance

NO PEEKING!

"... leave only your footprints..."

THE BLISTERS AND BLISS TEAM

DAVID FOSTER spends much of his trekking time checking out the flora and impressing others with his skill in building campfires and driftwood furniture. When he isn't chasing critters out of his backpack, David is a retired teacher and a nationally recognized gardener.

WAYNE AITKEN is frequently seen with his face in campfire smoke, tearfully preparing his culinary delights. His great pleasure is to follow in Dave's footsteps (particularly on sandy beaches). Between treks, Wayne tries desperately to keep his management consulting company afloat.

NELSON DEWEY is a cartoonist and illustrator. His work has appeared in numerous national magazines. He has illustrated over 30 outdoors and 'how to' books.

SPECIAL T-SHIRT OFFER

In response to at least three requests, we are making available a "Blisters and Bliss" T-Shirt – perfect for identifying yourself as a discriminating trekker.

FILL OUT A COPY OF THE FORM BELOW; enclose a cheque ("check" to our U.S. friends) or money order for $19.95 plus $3.00 shipping & handling – a total of $22.95 – and send to:

BLISTERS AND BLISS T-SHIRT
B&B Publishing
4081 San Capri Terrace
Victoria, B.C.,
CANADA V8N 2J6

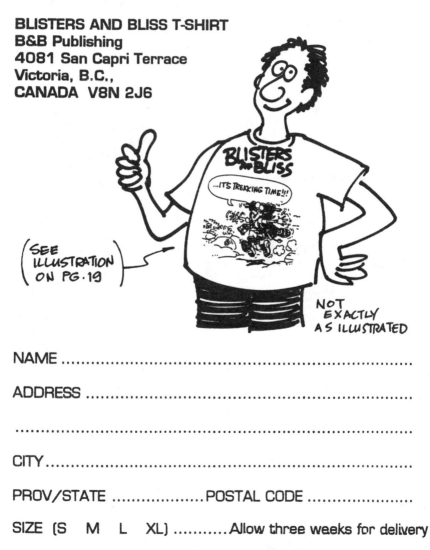

SEE ILLUSTRATION ON PG. 19

BLISTERS AND BLISS

...ITS TREKKING TIME!!!

NOT EXACTLY AS ILLUSTRATED

NAME ....

ADDRESS ....

....

CITY...

PROV/STATE ....POSTAL CODE ....

SIZE (S   M   L   XL) ....Allow three weeks for delivery